The
Winning Bid

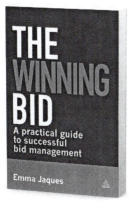

The Winning Bid

A practical guide to successful bid management

Emma Jaques

KoganPage

LONDON PHILADELPHIA NEW DELHI

First published in Great Britain and the United States in 2013 by Kogan Page Limited

120 Pentonville Road	1518 Walnut Street, Suite 1100	4737/23 Ansari Road
London N1 9JN	Philadelphia PA 19102	Daryaganj
United Kingdom	USA	New Delhi 110002
www.koganpage.com		India

© Emma Jaques, 2013

The right of Emma Jaques to be identified as the author of this work has been asserted by her in accordance with the Copyright, Designs and Patents Act 1988.

ISBN   978 0 7494 6832 3
E-ISBN   978 0 7494 6833 0

British Library Cataloguing-in-Publication Data

A CIP record for this book is available from the British Library.

Library of Congress Cataloging-in-Publication Data

Jaques, Emma.
  The winning bid : a practical guide to successful bid management / Emma Jaques. – 1st Edition.
    pages cm
  Includes bibliographical references and index.
  ISBN 978-0-7494-6832-3 – ISBN 978-0-7494-6833-0 (ebk.)   1. Proposal writing in business.
2. Letting of contracts.   I. Title.
  HF5718.5.J33 2013
  658.15'224–dc23
                                                                                          2012051531

Typeset by Graphicraft Limited, Hong Kong
Printed and bound in India by Replika Press Pvt Ltd

For Nick, Maddie and Josie

CONTENTS

FOREWORD

I spend a lot of my time delivering bid writing and management training courses, and one of the key questions I like to ask my delegates is 'Why does our customer want a bid?' The responses I get vary from delegate to delegate, but the more common responses include 'To make a comparison between firms', 'To get a good price' and 'To evaluate the best solution or offering'.

I'm more cynical than this. I believe that there is a more fundamental reason behind a customer's decision to go out to tender. I think the principal reason is because, if the chosen solution doesn't deliver, the decision makers can turn to their management and use the bid to justify their decision. They need your bid to protect their future.

Within the bid, you have to demonstrate that you can meet the customer's needs and provide proof. You have to tell the customer why it is safe to choose you.

I have a colleague who once lost a bid to the Ministry of Defence. The decision maker was a personal friend who knew that my colleague's company could deliver what the MOD was seeking. Unfortunately, the submitted bid didn't convey this message, and the job was awarded to an overseas company that ultimately failed to deliver. The decision maker nearly lost his job over the debacle. Imagine how angry the friend was, knowing that there was a UK company with the ability to do the work, but that he had to award the contract to an organization that went on to fail, jeopardizing his career – just on the strength of the written bid.

Buying is an emotional and logical process. Whether buying personally or professionally, we will always make the emotional decision first and then logically justify it. I like that car. Can I afford it? Can I get the kids into it? Will my spouse kill me if I buy it? We make all of our decisions in this way. It is exactly the same when we buy professionally, except that the professional buyer expects us to write the logical justification – the bid. We need to show what we can do and then do it.

So, when you next sit down to write a bid, remember that your customer needs a number of outcomes from it. The customer needs to know what you can do and how much it will cost, and is seeking proof that you can do it. You can be representing the best organization in the world, but you will not win business if your bid document doesn't demonstrate exactly what is possible through your proposed solution, safeguarding the customer and providing the customer with reassurance.

This book will help you to do just that.

Chris Milburn
Communications and PR Director
United Kingdom Association of Bid and
Proposal Management Professionals (UKAPMP)

ACKNOWLEDGEMENTS

It would be impossible to write a book like this without the input and support of lots of people along the way. I've worked on numerous bids, and with hundreds of bid contributors, all of whom have added to the experience I'm able to draw upon when writing. So thanks should firstly go to them.

There are some individuals, though, who truly deserve special thanks. Kate Long and Sue Dockerty, my colleagues at Onto the Page, have helped with research and ideas, and provide much-needed encouragement, especially when the going felt tough! My lovely friend and running partner Victoria Betton has also supported and encouraged me over the course of many miles and many months.

Thanks to David Magliano, who generously found time during his role as Director for the England 2018 World Cup bid to talk to me about the London 2012 bid. An inspiring experience!

To Chris Milburn, in his role as Marketing, PR and Communications Director of the UKAPMP, for writing the Foreword to this book, and giving me food for thought about bid terminology.

Jason Haigh and Jonny Hotchkiss at Design Junkie did my images – thanks, guys. Great stuff, as ever.

Many thanks to my fellow bid professionals and all who contributed to a discussion on 'where bids have gone wrong' on LinkedIn; it really made for interesting reading! I have included stories from the following contributors: Kevin French, Michael Gerner, James Michael Clewer, Chris Thompson, Gavin McGarty, Amanda Snee and Andrew Gittins. Thanks, everyone – great stories!

Biggest thanks of all go to my wonderful family, whose support and encouragement mean the world to me. Thanks, Mum, Dad, Lucy, Mike, Isaac, Eloise, Poppy, Vicki, Pete, Dan, Lucas, Billy, Marcus, Ian, Maria, Todd, Robbie and Oscar. You're the best!

And, of course, to my wonderful husband Nick, and my gorgeous daughters Maddie and Josie, who provide endless support and inspiration for everything I do.

Introduction

Managing bid and tender processes can be a daunting task, even for those with some experience in participating in them. This book is aimed at all who find themselves involved in bidding, from complete novices looking for step-by-step guidance to experienced bid managers looking for ideas to further improve their win rate.

In my day-to-day work as a bid consultant, I'm constantly asked for my advice or insight on bid-related matters, and I've tried to include the answers to all of the most frequently asked questions in this book. I've included some of my bidding experiences, gathered over the last 15 years (some positive, some downright depressing, others simply embarrassing). Reading this book will therefore help you to bypass the slog and get straight to the success!

Covering the full range of bid-related activities (including how to find opportunities in the first place), the book is written in a way that breaks down the process, giving practical, manageable advice at each step. As a result, the reader can easily dip in and out – accessing advice for specific issues and challenges as they are encountered. Also included are practical tools and techniques that don't rely on you having access to specialized systems, although there are signposts to these for the more advanced reader who might be ready to explore them.

It's not all about processes, though. The book gives an insight into what life is like for the bid manager's opposite number: the buyer. I spent time with a number of these elusive creatures, often perceived as the baddies of the piece, trying to understand what life is really like on the other side of the procurement divide. What emerged was quite surprising, and might even engender some feelings of sympathy amongst the bid community (OK, maybe not!). Either way, you'll be better informed about why buyers do what they do, and will be able to use this to your advantage in future.

There's a chapter that explores some real-life tendering stories, including my favourite: that of the bid for the London 2012 Olympic Games. Deemed as the underdogs of the competition, the London 2012 bid team managed to create a win theme that simply could not be ignored – a truly inspirational story for any aspiring bid manager. On the flip side, and for a bit of fun, I also cover some of those bids that didn't quite go to plan...

So there really is something for everyone who's engaged in the art of bidding. Whatever your own experience (or indeed lack of it), I hope that this book inspires you to create many winning bids in the future.

Best of luck!

Bid jargon explained – what it all means

When I meet people for the first time and I explain what I do, they always look a bit blank. I think it's the word 'bid' – it seems to conjure up an image of the auction room or even eBay in most people's minds. The word 'proposal' isn't much more illuminating. That seems to evoke images of romantic, down-on-one-knee invitations to tie the knot.

Within this book, I've tried to shy away from using too much jargon, although the use of some terms is embedded in the procurement and bidding world and is therefore unavoidable. To be honest, even within these worlds, there's not always a universal understanding or usage of certain words, phrases or terms.

What follows here, then, is my definition of the most commonly used terms that are to be found throughout this book, as well as some of the more baffling and specific terminology that you will be seeing as you read on.

Tenders, bids, proposals

Let's start with three of the most commonly used terms: tender, bid and proposal. What you'll actually find is that these three are used pretty inter-changeably: one person's bid is another's proposal, for instance. A buyer may issue an 'invitation to tender' or a 'request for proposal'. Same thing, different terminology.

However, for the purpose of this book, I'm going to pin things down a little more precisely – if only to try to make it a little easier to grasp. Just bear in mind that others might use these terms more loosely. So, within this book:

- A formal document issued by a customer, outlining a specific purchasing requirement and giving instructions about quoting for the work, is an **invitation to tender**, or simply a **tender document**.

- The written response document submitted by the supplier in response to the tender document is the **bid**.
- A sales document written by a supplier to a buyer without formal instructions to follow is a **proposal**.

Under my definition, then, from the supplier's perspective a bid is reactive, a proposal proactive. A bid will be a formal process, with competitors involved; a proposal may lead to a contract or an order without any other suppliers being engaged by the buyer. (Of course, sometimes a buyer will take the ideas included in a proposal and put them out to market, creating a tender/bid process.)

But there is one thing that bids and proposals definitely have in common. They are both trying to persuade the reader (that is, the buyer) to choose the given solution above any other possible option.

The buyer

Throughout the book I use the term 'buyer' to represent a single individual. I imagine the buyer as a representative of the buying organization: the procurement lead who directs the tendering process and makes the final recommendation to a board of directors.

The customer

I also refer to the buying organization as the 'customer', although 'client' would have been just as suitable.

Glossary of other frequently used terms

Terms are shown alphabetically.

Association of Bid and Proposal Management Professionals (APMP) Professional body for bid and proposal management professionals. Operating globally, with a thriving UK chapter.

benchmarking exercise A process whereby the buyer wishes to determine the market price for a particular contract and puts out a tender with a view to collecting information rather than actually making a contract award. Often used where there is a successful incumbent but the buyer wishes to drive down the incumbent's price.

common procurement vocabulary (CPV) codes   The codes that are used to classify an opportunity into the correct category within *OJEU*, so that suppliers can see which opportunities are most likely to relate to them. There are over 9,000 CPVs currently!

e-auction (also known as reverse auction)   Sometimes used at the end of the tendering process to drive costs down. Bidders have to enter their price online against others doing the same. The idea is that prices will reduce over the course of the auction, giving the best deal to the buyer.

expression of interest (EOI)   Often the first step in the bid process; buyers ask suppliers to let them know if they are interested in obtaining further information about a particular opportunity. In the public sector, you might need to provide some basic information about your company as part of this stage.

framework agreement   A process whereby a shortlist of suppliers is pre-selected by a buyer. Under the resulting agreement, if and when the buyer has a specific need, only these suppliers are then invited to quote.

freedom of information (FOI)   Legislation that allows access to government-held information.

funder (also known as funding body)   An organization willing to award funds for the advancement of a particular cause or purpose.

incumbent   The existing supplier; already delivering a product or service for the customer.

invitation to tender (ITT)   The formal document issued by a buyer that sets out the requirements for that opportunity. Contains instructions to potential bidders about how and when they need to submit their written response and costs. Normally only issued to a selected shortlist.

most economically advantageous tender (MEAT) (also known as best value)   The process of evaluating bids and selecting the one that offers the best value for money.

***Official Journal of the European Union* (*OJEU*)**   A central register for high-value contracts that are put out to tender by contracting authorities within the European Union. All opportunities over the current, prescribed EU thresholds must be advertised here.

pre-qualification questionnaire (PQQ)   A questionnaire issued by the buyer during a restricted procurement procedure, asking for information on finances, governance and experience, in the main. Allows a shortlist of suitable suppliers to be drawn up, who are then invited to participate in the next stage.

renewal   Process of bidding again for a contract that a supplier has won previously and is currently delivering.

request for information (RFI)   Similar to a PQQ, but only used in the private sector. Often used by buyers to request some details about the supplier's proposed solution for this opportunity as well as for shortlisting purposes.

request for proposal (RFP)   Interchangeable term with ITT.

request for quote (RFQ)   Like ITT and RFP, but focused towards the cost element.

value proposition   The demonstration of the overall benefit of a proposal, taking into consideration its cost.

win rate   The number of wins versus number of competitions entered. Normally expressed as a percentage or as a ratio of wins to bids submitted.

Bid basics
The fundamental things you need to know

01

THIS CHAPTER COVERS:

- The evolution of bidding

- Bid myths – truth or fiction?

- Skills analysis – what it takes to win a bid

Bidding is a great route to market, make no mistake. Yet many businesses shy away from seeking and pursuing opportunities procured via this route, and so miss out on lucrative contracts that they could definitely fulfil. Why? Because they perceive the process to be overly bureaucratic, or they think that they don't possess the right skills. They think that they don't have the time, or they simply don't know where to start. (I've heard loads of other reasons, but these seem to be the favourites.)

I want to show you what it takes to become a bid expert, and how your organization can benefit hugely from the array of opportunities that are put out to tender every year.

It really is a question of preparation and organization, and you can do it. In this chapter, we'll uncover the myths about bidding, so that all your ready-made excuses for not bidding are blown away. We'll explore where bidding opportunities can be found and how you can start to get noticed by buyers in both the public and the private sector.

And we'll look at the skills – and the mindset – you'll need to ensure that you win future bids. You'll be surprised that the skills required are not specialized, and that many of them already exist in your organization, however small it is.

The evolution of bidding

In days gone by, many contract deals were struck on the golf course, over a pint or over dinner. A quick chat about the work required, brief negotiation on price, handshake to seal the agreement. Done. (I realize this is somewhat of a generalization, and still happens to a certain extent, but you get the picture.)

With the advent of the European Union and legislation to ensure competition in the public sector, and the emergence of the procurement professional in the private sector, times have changed and will continue to do so.

Suppliers are increasingly required to enter into pre-contract competitions in order to secure new work, and in more and more cases this will be via a written submission. You are given instructions from the buyer in the form of a tender document; you follow them in order to create your bid. The bid tells the buyer what a supplier can do to meet the stated requirements, and how much the supplier will charge to do the work.

If, therefore, you wish to sell to the public sector, you are going to have to compete for the work by bidding for it. Similarly, the private sector is becoming more sophisticated in its procurement processes, and you are likely to be required to write bids or proposals in order to secure a contract. Alternatively, if you are a charity or not-for-profit organization seeking funding, you will more than likely need to prepare a compelling bid in order to secure the required grant.

The majority of this book covers the formal processes you'll need to follow when you are participating in any of these types of reactive bid competition (where there's a formal requirement to which you're required to respond). In addition, Chapter 13 gives advice on creating winning proactive proposals (by which I mean the document you create when someone says 'Send me something to tell me what you can do for me'). To be honest, there's a huge crossover between the two; if you can do one well, you can definitely do the other.

Bid myths – truth or fiction?

There are many myths and preconceptions about bids and bidding, many of them the reasons given for not participating. Maybe some of these will resonate with you; others might be new. The main thing you should take from this section is the idea that there are so many good reasons to bid and very few really good excuses not to!

Myth 1: Tenders are only issued to big businesses, for big contracts

Fiction. Since the publication of the Gershon Review way back in 2004, which looked at public sector efficiency and spending, much has been done to change the culture of public procurement. As a result, attitudes towards buying from small and medium-size enterprises (SMEs) have altered significantly. In recognition of the fact that small businesses can offer agility, flexibility, commitment and specialist skills to buyers, much has been done to bring these parties together.

Most recently, the UK government, via the Cabinet Office, is doing much to ensure public sector buyers meet the given target: that 25 per cent of all public sector contracts should be awarded to SMEs. (By the way, the EU defines the upper limits of SMEs as being those with fewer than 250 employees or with a turnover of less than €50 million.) With an estimated £150 billion being spent in the UK on public sector contracts annually, that's a very tasty slice of the cake for small and medium-sized business.

If 25 per cent sounds somewhat ambitious, it is heartening that some action is at least being taken to 'level the playing field' when it comes to smaller companies competing with their mega-competitors.

For a start, the UK's Cabinet Office has appointed a Crown commercial representative (no less) for smaller SMEs. Stephen Allott, a barrister and technology entrepreneur by trade, has pledged to act as a champion for the interests of this group, and some interesting activities have already taken place. Furthermore, there are also tangible efforts at simplifying pre-qualification processes (or, for smaller contracts, even removing the need for these processes altogether), so that SMEs don't fall *before* the first hurdle (you'll find more on the practicalities of this in Chapter 3).

Then there's the move to split bigger contracts into 'micro-lots': those that even the smallest supplier could fulfil. In tandem with this, larger firms are encouraged to subcontract to their smaller counterparts.

In addition, there's the Cabinet Office's 'mystery shopper' initiative that encourages SMEs to report procurement processes that are unfairly weighted against them. Since its launch in February 2011, a number of procurement processes have been revised, reworked or even restarted; you can read about specific cases at the Cabinet Office website (see **http://www.cabinetoffice.gov. uk/resource-library/mystery-shopper-results**).

There is also a move to promote ready access to 'lower-value' contracts: those below the given EU thresholds, details of which are covered in Chapter 2. In recognition that many small and medium-sized businesses are well placed to compete for such opportunities (valued above £113,000 or €130,000), the government is trying to increase access in a number of ways, principally through its e-portal, Contracts Finder, which is also covered in detail in Chapter 2.

Even when the contract is deemed higher-value, and is published on a register called the *Official Journal of the European Union (OJEU)*, some are only just over the thresholds – they're not all multimillion-pound deals.

In Chapter 2 we'll explore exactly how to go about finding public sector opportunities, and how processes are designed to ensure fair and competitive procurement.

In the private sector, buyers looking for the best deal will often issue an ITT or RFP to selected suppliers to see who can provide the best solution at the best price. Sometimes these can be for very small pieces of work; the smallest private sector contract I have bid for was worth less than £1,000. The trick in this sector is getting yourself known to buyers in the first place, so that you're on their list when they come to issue the tender documents.

So there's plenty to go at for businesses of every size, from the smallest to the largest. In Chapter 2 we'll explore exactly how to get yourself in a position to participate in private and public sector competitions, whatever your company's size.

Myth 2: Most bid processes are fixed, with a winner identified before the start

Partially true. In the private sector, this myth might have a grain of truth to it, especially in competitions where there is an incumbent. In these instances, other bidders are always suspicious that this might be a benchmarking exercise, designed to drive down the incumbent's price. Worse still, they feel that their bid might be used as free consultancy: the buyer having no intention of letting the contract to another supplier, but interested in an injection of fresh ideas. You'll have to decide whether this is the case for any of your opportunities, and act accordingly.

If this were true in the public sector, it would be anti-competitive and illegal, for a start. Public sector buyers go to great lengths to ensure that processes are open, fair and equitable. That's not to say that they don't have opinions and preferences that they are sometimes looking to verify in a bid process. But, with the advent of the EU regulations and of freedom of information legislation, buyers have to be prepared for their decisions to be publicly scrutinized, and are very firm about sticking to the rules.

Myth 3: You need to have special skills to complete a bid, and I don't have them

Fiction. It's true that larger businesses are more likely to have in-house bid teams whose core responsibility is to identify new opportunities and to lead the sales process from qualification through to win. It therefore follows that these teams have specialist tools and skills to help them to achieve their targets. However, it's probably also true that they are competing for high-value, complex contracts that need a professional bid approach to ensure that the deals are designed correctly and presented well.

However, if you are running a small business and are therefore perhaps bidding to provide a local service, do you need the same skills as the big operators? You'll be glad to hear that the answer is no. You need time and resource to bid, and you must be sure that your proposition is deliverable, winnable and profitable (more of this in Chapter 4). Other than that, you need a pragmatic approach, endless enthusiasm for what you're proposing, an ability to think about things from the buyer's perspective, and the determination to present your solution in the best possible light. If you've got all of these and you're prepared to follow the advice contained in this book, I reckon you're in with a very good chance of winning.

Myth 4: I don't need to do much; a company brochure and a few lines about how we generally do things should be sufficient

Fiction. There really is no point in submitting a bid that looks like this; I can almost guarantee that it won't win. Even when you're selling a commodity rather than a service, buyers often look for the way in which a supplier does business as a differentiating factor, especially when prices are identical or very close.

Participating in a bid is an all-or-nothing activity. Give it the time and attention it needs, or use the time more constructively elsewhere in your business.

Myth 5: Bids are really hard work, take ages and are overly bureaucratic

Partially true – sorry! I am certainly not going to pretend that bidding for new business is easy or always straightforward. But it is manageable, even by non-experts. Mostly, it's just a question of familiarizing yourself with the language used and the rules that are given. Take the time to understand what is required, and you're less likely to trip over the 'red tape' side of things. And if you conduct a lessons learnt session at the end of a bid process, you're going to be in much better shape the next time. Furthermore, if you store the information you've created in some sort of knowledge base, your next bid will be much faster to complete.

Skills analysis – what it takes to win a bid

You may now be a little more open to the idea of your organization being able to find opportunities for which to bid, but perhaps your original doubt remains: do you have the expertise you need to write a winning bid?

Perhaps if we explore the overall skills that you'll need, you can begin to convince yourself that this just might be possible, because actually attitude is just as important as skills when participating in a bid, and the skills that you need are the ones that keep any good business running well:

Attitude	Skills
Commitment	Time and resource management
Customer focus	Commercial awareness
Passion	Team working
Energy	Good written communication skills
Determination	The ability to complete a detailed task

If you can tick off each of the above, then I promise you that you're in good shape to compete for new business through bids. There really isn't a magic formula, although there are some golden rules.

You'll need some tools – but again, to start with, nothing more than your office is doubtless already equipped with. Later, as you become more confident and ambitious in your bidding career, you'll perhaps want to invest in some speciality bidding tools or systems.

So, if you're prepared to give it everything (and it really does have to be all or nothing, I'm afraid), then read on. You're now ready to understand the process by which your inherent skills, your positive attitude and your organization's unique offering can come together to win you a bid competition.

SUMMARY

Bidding is not a quick or easy route to market, but if you understand and follow the rules it can be very rewarding. There's no need to invest in specialist tools at the start of your bid journey – the right attitude and skills are much more important if you're going to participate successfully in bid competitions. Find the people in your organization who are the most suitable to help you bid to win, and support them wholeheartedly!

Where to look for bidding opportunities

02

THIS CHAPTER COVERS:

- Finding public sector opportunities
- Finding private sector opportunities

Of course, to be able to participate in a bid competition, you need to know about it in the first place. For many companies, this is the first stumbling block; they just don't know how to find a way in.

Admittedly, in the private sector it can feel like a closed shop – if you're not proactive. But if you are prepared to engage with your target customers, to talk to them and to understand them, you'll find more and more doors open to you.

Strangely, in the public sector it can feel as though the opposite is true – there's so much information about contracts that are up for tender that it can be difficult to identify the ones that are right for you. Let's look at that conundrum next, then.

Finding public sector opportunities

Before we explore just how to take advantage of public sector opportunities, it's important to understand how public sector contracts are procured and why things are done this way. I introduced the concept of lower- and higher-value contracts in Chapter 1. Now we need to explore the legislation that exists and how it dictates exactly how opportunities are classified as either lower or higher, and therefore procured.

The relevant pieces of legislation are the Public Contracts Regulations 2006 (amended 2009), which cover England, Wales and Northern Ireland, and the Public Contracts (Scotland) Regulations 2012, which cover, not surprisingly, Scotland.

Any opportunity with a lifetime contract value (net of VAT) below a certain threshold is not bound fully by these regulations. Everything with a contract value above the threshold is bound by them. Let's look at the cut-off points and see what this means in practice.

Public sector contract thresholds

The thresholds are reviewed and set by the European Union (and are therefore in euros) every two years. A simplified summary of the current thresholds (last revised in January 2012) is shown in Table 2.1.

To find more detail about the different bodies to which the thresholds relate, and for the precise definition of supplies, services and works, you'll need to

TABLE 2.1   EU thresholds from January 2012

Contracting authority	'Supplies' threshold (goods, commodities, etc)	'Services' threshold	'Works' threshold (construction, civil engineering projects, etc)
Certain central government bodies (as listed in the Regulations)	£113,057 (€130,000)	£113,057 (€130,000)	£4,348,350 (€5,000,000)
All other public sector contracting authorities	£173,934 (€200,000)	£173,934 (€200,000)	£4,348,350 (€5,000,000)
Small lots	£69,574 (€80,000)	£69,574 (€80,000)	£869,670 (€1,000,000)

SOURCE: www.ojec.com.
NOTE: For the 'services' threshold, some exceptions apply.

read the Public Contracts Regulations 2006 (amended 2009) documentation, which is freely available on the internet.

But don't worry too much about the detail of this. What you really need to know is that a buyer will tackle the tendering process differently depending on whether the opportunity is above or below the threshold.

Oh, and by the way, buyers can divide a contract into 'lots', but no more than 20 per cent of the whole contract can be let this way. And even then the threshold for 'small lots' is currently £69,574, or €80,000. This is to ensure that buyers don't simply slice up the contract into small enough pieces to fall below the threshold and avoid the regulations.

If the buyer calculates that the opportunity is above the threshold, the regulations will apply as long as a couple of other preconditions are met (again, for the detail of this, please see the regulations documentation). The buyer will then need to advertise the opportunity in the *Official Journal of the European Union (OJEU)* and follow the procedures that the regulations set out.

If the buyer calculates that the opportunity is below the threshold, the regulations do not apply to the same extent. The buyer must still 'adequately advertise' the opportunity, after deciding whether it is likely to be of interest to suppliers locally, nationally or even EU-wide. The buyer must do so in a way that promotes competition, although there are no hard-and-fast rules about how buyers should actually go about this. The important things to note are that they are not allowed to be passive in the process (simply waiting for suppliers to contact them) and they do not need to use *OJEU* to advertise a below-threshold contract opportunity.

Finding lower-value public sector opportunities

We know that buyers need to 'adequately advertise' lower-value contracts, but what exactly does this mean?

The best approach when researching supply routes to target organizations is the direct one. Ring them up and ask to speak to the procurement or buying function. Ask how they engage with suppliers and where they advertise lower-value contracts. Hopefully you will find them receptive; it's their job to keep abreast of the marketplace, and a good buying team will want to keep 'scanning the market' for good suppliers.

What you will probably find is that different contracting authorities will have different policies below the thresholds. Often they will have an approved supplier list (see the box below), so you'll need to find out how to get on it. Such a list will allow them to request a quote or to put out a tender without the need to advertise to the market.

Approved supplier lists

Buyers often run approved supplier lists (sometimes known as preferred supplier lists or PSLs) to simplify and speed up the buying process. An approved supplier is one that has been pre-qualified by the buyer, and is deemed to be suitable and capable for relevant future contracts. Some sort of formal selection process will take place, normally outside of a time when any live tenders are available. The prize at the end of the selection process is not a contract but a place on a shortlist of suppliers. When contracts do come up for tender, only the approved suppliers will be invited to submit a quote or bid.

Such a process will allow the buyer to demonstrate that contracts are being competitively let without having to go through a shortlisting process each time.

Some authorities have 'open' preferred supplier lists, and will accept applications at any time. Others have 'closed' lists and invite applications only at fixed intervals. These usually vary from 12 months to three years.

In other cases, buyers will use a regional procurement website on which to publicize their smaller contracts. Find out which one is used by the public body you'd like to supply, and sign up to it. Buyers might use their own organization's website, so look for a 'tenders' section, bookmark it and then visit it regularly (at least once a week). They might also use the local or national press or relevant trade journals to advertise tenders.

There's a strong chance, however, that they'll be using one of two national portals to publicize their below-threshold opportunities: Contracts Finder or Supply Contracts.

Contracts Finder

Contracts Finder (**www.contractsfinder.businesslink.gov.uk/**) is the UK government's own portal, access to which is free. It allows you to:

- search for public sector (only) opportunities valued over £10,000 (it also carries above-threshold opportunities);
- see a 'pipeline' of intended/possible future procurement activity;
- find out who has been awarded contracts (although only information from October 2010 onwards is available via this site);
- see current tender and contract information.

This should definitely be your first port of call in your pursuit of new public sector contracts. You can even subscribe to a daily alert service that sends you, by e-mail, a summary of the opportunities against criteria that you have selected.

Obviously, you will need to get to know Contracts Finder like the back of your hand, taking the time to set up your search criteria correctly, making sure you visit it regularly to check for new opportunities, or reading your alert e-mails daily. You can even set up a profile to promote your organization, to which buyers have access. Sometimes, buyers will use the supplier profile facility to find suitable suppliers to invite to tender. This is also the case when main contractors, who have already been awarded a public sector contract, are looking for subcontractors.

Supply Contracts

Supply Contracts, often referred to simply as 'Supply' (**www.supplycontracts. co.uk/**), is a commercial portal also publicizing below- and above-threshold opportunities. You can register free for local opportunities, but if you want to access regional or national listings you will be required to pay a fee.

Other useful resources for searching for lower-value opportunities also exist; sometimes buyers prefer a category- or industry-specific portal on which to advertise their tenders. A few useful examples of this are shown in Table 2.2.

TABLE 2.2   Lower-value opportunities websites

Website	Purpose
www.bluelight.gov.uk	For national emergency services tenders
www.constructionline.co.uk	For construction tenders
www.supply2health.nhs.uk	For lower-value clinical (NHS Part B) tenders
http://www.supplychain.nhs.uk/ suppliers/procurement- opportunities/	For consumables and clinical product tenders
http://gps.cabinetoffice.gov.uk/ i-am-supplier/register-future- opportunities	The Dynamic Marketplace: a request for quotation (RFQ) service for government contracts
https://www.competefor.com	For public projects (includes subcontracting opportunities)

It might be worth noting here that there is a range of fee-charging companies that offer public sector tender searching services. These are ideal if you're short of time and resource for this task, and want someone to look through the alerts from all the available national and regional registers on your behalf.

Finding higher-value opportunities

Where a public sector contract exceeds the relevant threshold, the buyer is bound by the regulations and has no choice but to advertise via *OJEU*. Mandatory templates are used and standard common procurement vocabulary (CPV) codes selected to classify the notice so that suppliers can easily find it. In theory, all you need to do is to search on the Tenders Electronic Daily (TED) website (**http://ted.europa.eu**) to find those notices classified within your specialist field.

However, it's universally accepted that finding the right opportunities using only CPV codes is pretty hard, even after the whole system was overhauled in 2003. Buyers and suppliers often have different notions of which codes apply. Supplementary codes are supposed to help buyers to classify more precisely under a main code – but often they are not used, and suppliers have to search through many notices to find what's relevant.

Just to show you what I mean, a buyer looking for printing services could choose from:

79800000-2	Printing and related services
79810000-5	Printing services
9820000-8	Services related to printing
79823000-9	Printing and delivery services
79824000-6	Printing and distribution services

Which would be the right choice? Of course, when you, as a print supplier, start searching the journal, you have to look through all these codes (and many more) to make sure you haven't missed any potentially relevant notices. Needles/haystacks spring to mind.

Just as an aside, a skip through the complete list of CPV codes (see 'Electronic sources' in the References for a link) throws up some interesting ideas. For instance, how often do you think code 92332000-7, 'Beach services', gets used? And how many high-value contracts need code 92342200-2, 'Discotheque dance-instruction services'?

So you can see the system is a good idea, just difficult to navigate (maybe it loses something in translation?). In short, trying to set up your preferences and navigate TED can be time-consuming and quite frustrating, but it is free!

As an alternative, you might find that one of the fee-charging agencies can help you find your way around *OJEU* more successfully. A quick search on the internet under 'tender alerts' will find you the main players.

Other routes to public sector contracts

Government Procurement Service (GPS)

The GPS is an executive agency of the Cabinet Office. Essentially, it provides a procurement service to the public sector, through which buyers can pay a transaction fee to access the benefits of the large framework agreements that are running under the centralized procurement strategy. This includes frameworks for health and the wider public sector. A framework agreement is essentially a grander version of the approved supplier list model, allowing appropriate suppliers to be pre-identified for above-threshold contracts.

The GPS acts on behalf of the contracting authorities, by putting out framework agreements to tender on their behalf. Because of the size of the potential contracts (some of these are *huge*), these framework tenders are first published via *OJEU*. Bidders are competing for a place on a shortlist for a set period, not for a specific contract. Once shortlisted, suppliers may then be asked to submit additional tenders via the GPS eSourcing site against an actual requirement. The GPS process is stringent and can be very time-consuming, with no guarantee of any actual work at the end of it. Be sure that you are clear what you are letting yourself in for before setting off down this road.

Government eMarketplace – the Dynamic Marketplace

Also run by the GPS, the Dynamic Marketplace e-portal was launched in 2011 to 'ensure that government procurement is easily accessible to all suppliers, including small and medium enterprises'.

It exists to put suppliers and public sector buyers together for below-threshold opportunities or those of low complexity. Once registered (you'll need to post a profile), in theory, buyers will be able to contact you to request a quote, and you won't need to submit a full bid. Buyers pay a transaction fee on a sliding scale; suppliers are not charged. This resource can be found at **https://buyers.procserveonline.com/otis/preregistration/splash_page.html**.

'Meet the buyer' events

Another very useful route to public sector buyers is through the regional or industry-specific 'meet the buyer' events staged by chambers of commerce and other organizations around the country (occasionally you will come across similar, private sector events, especially for large capital projects that require a significant element of subcontracting). These events offer you the opportunity to talk directly to procurement professionals, to find out about future competitions and approved supplier processes. They also allow you to hear at first hand about the dos and don'ts of bidding – from those poor people who have to read bids for a living! As a bidder, you should view these events as an absolute priority, and attend them whenever possible.

Types of procurement processes in the public sector

There are four types of procurement procedures for above-threshold opportunities, and it's useful to understand which is relevant to a tender before you embark on its completion. The type of procedure can have a huge bearing on the work you'll be required to undertake – and on the likelihood of you winning. The four are open, restricted, competitive dialogue and negotiated.

Open

This type of procedure is normally used for the purchase of commodities or where the requirement is not complex. Under this procedure, every interested party that wishes to submit a bid will be allowed to do so. The bidder will first be evaluated against the contracting authority's selection criteria, and only if bidders successfully pass this stage will their bid be evaluated.

Essentially, under an open procedure, the shortlist and bid evaluation processes happen at the same time. The buyer cannot subsequently negotiate with bidders (although the buyer can request clarification on any aspect of the bid(s) received), but must accept one (or more) of the offers submitted – or restart the process. Open procedures will often attract high numbers of bidders and can therefore be very difficult to win.

A procedure very similar to the one described above is often used for below-threshold opportunities, too. It's just that the regulations don't apply to these smaller opportunities, and so there can be some variance in the process deployed by the buyer.

Restricted

Anyone interested in bidding within a restricted procedure can express an interest, but must successfully pass through a selection process (often termed 'pre-qualification' – see Chapter 3) before being invited to tender. Tenders will then be evaluated against pre-advised evaluation criteria. As with the open procedure, negotiation with bidders is not permitted within a restricted procedure.

Restricted procedures are the most common form of procurement process. In a way, they at least mean that bidders don't have to complete the entire process only to find out that they were never even considered for the contract, owing to their failure to meet one or more of the selection criteria. On the other hand, a two-stage process can be very time-consuming – although moves are being made to simplify, or at least unify, the first (pre-qualification) part of the process. The cynic in me thinks that, even if the pre-qualification stage is easier, it will only transfer the pain to the next stage: more bidders = more competition = even harder to win! There are no easy solutions when you start with a long list of interested suppliers.

Competitive dialogue

A relatively uncommon procedure, competitive dialogue is used for larger, more complex contracts for which the buyer is seeking input from potential suppliers in order to shape the eventual solution. Potential bidders must first pre-qualify against given selection criteria before receiving specification documents and being invited to participate in face-to-face dialogue.

Once the dialogue is under way, each bidder will meet directly with the contracting authority's buying team at formal meetings, to discuss the specification and potential solutions. Ideas, innovations and proposals are invited by the bidder, to allow the optimum solution to be created. Bidders might be required to document solutions between dialogue meetings, before submitting their final proposal at the end of the dialogue schedule. The best proposal is then selected, but there is then only limited scope for any further negotiation or amendment with the preferred bidder.

Competitive dialogue can be used only under the circumstances described in the regulations.

My experience of competitive dialogue

You don't come across competitive dialogue procedures too often. I've been 'lucky' enough to have been involved in a few tenders that have followed this process, and each one certainly was an experience!

The first one I ever worked on never even made it to contract award. Our bid team realized that the contracting authority's requirements simply could not be met – and other bidders were telling them the same thing. This emerged as part of the dialogue, and eventually the buyer withdrew the process. Unfortunately it took three stages of dialogue, two written submissions and six months to arrive at that stage.

The other notable example was a much more successful dialogue. This time, the procedure undoubtedly ensured that the contracting authority received a more innovative, efficient and cost-effective bid than a restricted process would have secured. It's just a shame it took almost three years from start to finish...

If you are involved in a competitive dialogue process, be prepared for it to take longer than under other procedures. Also, don't expect the dialogue to be free and open! In my experience, the actual 'dialogue' is fairly one-sided. So make sure you're prepared for your time in front of the procurement team. It might feel as though your audience is impassive, but you will often see your ideas, innovations and indeed concerns reflected in revised specifications when information relating to the next stage of the process is published. So take the opportunity to state your developing case and don't be deterred by the silence!

Negotiated

There are two types of the negotiated procedure; these can be used only in very limited circumstances, as described in the regulations.

Under the first type ('without prior advert'), the contracting authority is not required to issue an *OJEU* notice, even if it is above the threshold, and is permitted to negotiate directly with the supplier of its choice.

Under the second ('with prior advert'), the authority must publish an *OJEU* notice. Following a pre-qualification phase for all interested parties, bidders are then invited to negotiate the terms of the advertised contract. The authority will then make an award based on the negotiations.

In both of the above cases, the regulations do not specify the procedures for the actual negotiation.

All of the relevant resources introduced in this section can be found via the internet. See 'Electronic sources' in the References for all the relevant links.

Finding private sector opportunities

Much as I'd like to be able to tell you about a central register of private sector opportunities, I'm afraid I can't, because it just doesn't exist. There are some tender alert agencies offering a limited service in this regard, but very few opportunities get recorded via this route. Since there's no law compelling private sector buyers to publicize their tender processes (and we've explored how tough it is for the public sector buyer to arrive at a shortlist), why would they?

So it's down to you to get yourself known to buyers and other decision makers within companies you've identified as potential customers. Your aim is to be on a preferred supplier list or on their long or shortlist of potential suppliers.

This requires a strategic approach – sometimes known as 'capture planning' in bidding circles. Although that sounds like management-speak, it simply refers to your plan of action for capturing this client and becoming a supplier to the client in the future.

Capture planning

Capture planning is an ongoing activity; you should constantly be working towards the goal of engagement with prospective clients. Your capture plan will help you to manage this more easily (otherwise it can feel like an insurmountable task).

Start with a target list of perhaps 10 organizations that you'd love to work with. Be realistic. Keep the list fresh; don't be afraid to strike names from the list as your capture plan proceeds – or succeeds!

Next, document your capture plan for each target. This can be as formal or as informal as you like, but to make life easier for yourself record everything you've discovered about the target company in one place. The idea is that the picture you build will be of great use not only to 'capture' the prospect, but also during the bidding processes that you subsequently participate in. Your understanding of their vision, challenges, people, processes and plans, plus, of course, their attitude to buying and outsourcing, will be invaluable in the bidding phase. Information gathered during your capture planning phase is rarely wasted.

Make it your mission to raise awareness of your offering with the right people (we'll explore who these might be, below) in each of your target organizations:

- Start with the easy stuff – check your target's website regularly so that you can build up a picture of their activity over time. Specifically look for annual reports, press releases or other strategic documents that set out the company's vision, values, objectives and aims in the short, medium and long term. (Don't forget you're aiming to build up a picture of how your product or service can benefit them, and how your values are complementary to their own – all of this knowledge will help to show your alignment to their own goals and working culture.)

- Look out for stories about them in the news so that you can understand their challenges and successes. Ideally, look for sources other than the target's own website; third-party sources will probably give a more realistic idea of their issues. Try to envisage a way that your product or service could help them to overcome a particular challenge or an immediate or future problem.

- Try to establish the identities of the key people in the organization – by that I mean those who might be receptive to your 'advances' and with whom you might be able to open a useful dialogue. Such people might include strategic managers whose wider team might benefit from your product or service, potential first-hand users of the product or service, and, of course, buyers or procurement people. Of course, you might have to find your 'in' through various means, and will certainly have to pass internal gatekeepers. LinkedIn (see below) and other social networking sites do make this a little easier!

- Once you've got a good feel for who the key people are and how they might possibly benefit from working with you, work to establish a no-obligation dialogue with them – there's no need to go into full sales mode initially. In fact it might be better if you state your intention: 'We'd love to work with you in the future. We're not trying to sell to you just now – just want to know what we'd need to do to become a supplier of yours...' Aim to build a 'power map', so that you understand who's who in your target company – and always be on the lookout for onward introductions from existing contacts.

- So, to that end, create a profile on LinkedIn (**www.Linkedin.com**) for yourself and your organization, and invite the key people in your target organizations to join your professional network. If you keep your profile up to date, your contacts will receive regular snippets of information about what you're up to. This can be subtle but effective marketing – especially if you can persuade existing customers to recommend your work. Also ask if you can put key people on your mailing list, and send them case studies and a link to your website.

- Try to attend events and seminars that you know they'll go to (and talk to them there, of course!).

All of the above will help you to create a complete picture of your target customer, and will increase their awareness of you.

Of course, your general marketing approach will also be vital in creating awareness of your presence in the market, and I recommend that you actively maintain as much activity as you can in this regard. You should aim to be recognized as an expert in your field (however competitive it may be), so that buyers automatically include you on their list (be it long or short) when they first put a tender out to the marketplace.

I'd especially recommend that you consider the following:

- Thought leadership activities – try to get speaker engagements at relevant trade events, so that people start to think of you or your organization as an influencer in your field.

- Awards – seek opportunities for independent recognition through awards. They are great PR vehicles. Best of all, you can put your new-found bidding skills into creating your award submissions, since the majority of the bid 'tricks' you'll learn in this book will be of great use in award writing too.

- Networking – take every opportunity to meet potential buyers via networking events. Your local chamber of commerce views the staging of such events as one its core objectives. Make the most of their services.

- Quality accreditations – although themselves a huge investment in time and resources, quality accreditations can provide a massive benefit to suppliers in bid competitions. Indeed, some buyers will stipulate a particular accreditation as an entry requirement: if you don't have it, you won't progress beyond the initial qualification stage. For further information about accreditations and which might be right for you, visit the International Organization for Standardization (ISO) website at **www.iso.org/iso/home.htm,** or the United Kingdom Accreditation Service (UKAS) website at **www.ukas.com**.

Bear in mind that each of the capture plan suggestions shown above for private sector buyers works equally well with public sector buyers.

Where buyers look for suppliers

Whenever I meet private sector buyers (outside of a bid situation, of course), I like to ask them one of my 'pet' questions – how do you arrive at a long list for your tender process, from which to select your shortlist? They each have their own unique response, of course, but some major themes generally crop up; these are explored below – along with advice on how to exploit them.

Existing suppliers

It's no surprise to learn that a supplier's successful past relationship with the buying organization is a great advantage for future deals. A good track record will pretty much guarantee your place in the next round of tendering. But don't be complacent. Buyers don't much like the 'cosy' relationship that can be created between those that use a product or service internally and those that supply it. It's their job to create some tension when the contract is up for renewal, to ensure best value is derived from the renegotiations.

Discussion with colleagues (particularly technical, operational and end-users of the product or service being commissioned)

Creating a good specification for the specific procurement in hand is one of the principal tasks a buyer needs to undertake. As a result, the buyer will need to work very closely with those people within the buying organization who will use the product or service, to ensure that the specification is clear and delivers what these internal users really need. It is likely that these 'specifiers' will have strong opinions on how the contract should be delivered – and who the buyer 'should' include in the procurement process. So it makes sense that you should be aiming to develop relationships with specifiers in your target organizations as well as buyers.

Internet search

Many buyers admit to browsing the web when looking for new suppliers – they can do so without experiencing a hard sell, and they can collect ideas from case studies and other information provided. Other books will give you advice about marketing yourself effectively via the internet. All I'm saying is that a strong web presence is vital for attracting private sector buyers, and that they do much of their research this way. So make sure that, if they find you via an internet search, your website encourages them to take their interest further.

Purchase of lists

The increasing sophistication of search engines means that this is becoming less popular as an option, but you do come across the occasional buyer who still likes to go to a specialist data agency, requesting a tailored list of potential suppliers.

Professional bodies

Buyers will often start their search at the professional body, and your presence in this channel could be a good source of leads. If your sector has one, it's always worth investigating the benefits that membership of a professional body can bring you – including this one!

Buyer–supplier brokerage sites

There are a number of sites that exist to broker relationships between private sector buyers and suppliers. In the main, buyers get free access to the information; it's the suppliers who have to pay to be listed, although this is not always the case. The idea is that suppliers showcase themselves and the products and services that they supply via their profile, and that buyers can browse these profiles to find suitable potential suppliers.

The biggest of such sites is Achilles (**www.achilles.com**). With a worldwide reach, they specialize in providing procurement services in the construction, ICT, oil and gas, transport and utilities sectors. If you wish to supply a buying organization that uses Achilles, then you'll have to register with the site and proceed through their accreditation process in order to do so. There's a charge for this service; it's tailored to the size of your organization and the part(s) of the Achilles service you access. Where you have, or are forming, a relationship with a buying organization that uses Achilles, this fee can be a useful (perhaps vital) investment. If you are signing up simply in the hope that a buyer will find you via this route, it's a much less certain return on that investment. All I'll say is that currently, on the Achilles site, they claim to work with 700 buying organizations and 55,000 suppliers. That's a lot of suppliers per buyer!

Of course, other sites, operating on a similar principle, are available. If you're going to invest time and money in these, be sure to quiz them about the results they achieve for organizations similar to yours before you commit. And make sure you understand the terms of your participation; some brokers charge you a percentage commission if you win a contract you first found via them. You definitely want to know about this up front.

If you follow the capture planning model, you should find yourself at least on a long list of suppliers within some of your target organizations. The next step, of course, is to be included in actual tender processes. We'll look at this next step (and similarly how to pre-qualify in the public sector) in the next chapter.

SUMMARY

There are very different rules for buyers in the public and private sectors. Make sure you're familiar with procurement processes within your target organizations.

The public sector has to engage fully with the market, and central public sector registers make it much easier to find opportunities relevant to your offering. (However, this does mean that public sector processes are extremely competitive.) Get signed up to the appropriate registers right away, and ensure that you carry out frequent searches so that you don't miss anything.

On the other hand, private sector opportunities are less easy to find and to be invited to participate in. However, if you are invited, you'll start the process on a shorter list of potential suppliers. There are lots of ways you can start to engage with potential buyers and create advantage for your organization in future opportunities. Start planning your targeted campaign immediately.

Capture planning, the art of targeting new customers, is an ongoing activity, and you should make the time to carry out some form of activity aimed at bringing you closer to a live opportunity with your target organizations every week. This is as true in the public sector as it is in the private sector.

Pre-qualifying for tenders
The first hurdle

03

THIS CHAPTER COVERS:

- Public sector pre-qualification

- Private sector shortlisting

In competitive markets, buyers are faced with the very real prospect of being overwhelmed with interested bidders should they simply publicize an opportunity to all-comers. This is equally true of buyers in both the private and the public sector. How do they identify the best offer amongst so many suppliers?

This, of course, is the fundamental role of the procurement professional, but that doesn't mean it's easy. More often than not, they are faced with a huge potential pool of suppliers, unless they are purchasing specialist goods or a truly niche product or service.

In both sectors, buyers would ideally like a shortlist of suppliers with whom to engage, and subsequently to invite to tender. But how they go about drawing up this shortlist is fundamentally different in the two sectors. In Chapter 2, we explored how to find bidding opportunities in both the public and the private sector. As part of this, we looked at how private sector buyers decide on which potential suppliers to include in their long lists.

We also looked at the various types of procurement procedures deployed by the public sector; in all of them except the open procedure (and the first type of negotiated procedure), there is a need to undertake some kind of selection process to arrive at a manageable long list of suppliers who will then be invited to tender. This is known as pre-qualification, and often requires you to complete a pre-qualification questionnaire (PQQ).

If you are going to succeed in bidding, it is vital to understand how to get over the shortlisting or pre-qualification hurdle, often the highest in the whole process. This chapter covers precisely this task. Let's start, as before, with the public sector.

Public sector pre-qualification

Expressing interest

The first thing you're likely to need to do, before even the pre-qualification stage, is to 'express an interest' in the contract opportunity that you've found.

As you'll see as you look through the tendering registers, there is normally very little detail included in the notice about the actual requirements of the contract. In most cases, there are just one or two sentences giving only the briefest outline of the product or service the buyer wishes to procure.

Unless there are other instructions within the notice, to express interest normally means e-mailing the contact given, and advising them that you are interested in receiving further details about the opportunity. You will sometimes see this referred to as the expression of interest (EOI) stage.

You will then receive back some additional information about the contract requirements and, usually, a pre-qualification questionnaire (PQQ). Once you have these you'll be able to begin to assess whether the opportunity looks suitable for your organization, and to get an indication of the process the buyer is running. But even by now you won't have all the information required to make a final decision about bidding. Only those successfully navigating the PQQ process will be invited to tender and receive the full tender documents. And it's only at *that* stage that you'll be able to assess fully whether or not you should go ahead and participate in the bid competition. But first you'll need to complete your PQQ in order to make it onto the shortlist of those invited to tender.

What form will the PQQ take?

Traditionally, there has been a huge variety of PQQs used; pretty much each contracting authority designed and used its own form and selection criteria to determine who should be invited to tender. PQQs need initially to establish the capability and credibility of the potential bidders, as well as their capacity and financial stability. Often a contracting authority uses the same questionnaire regardless of what it is procuring, and you find yourself answering some seemingly bizarre and irrelevant questions that simply do not relate to your area of work.

The Cabinet Office of the UK government has recognized that this puts off many smaller companies, which simply don't bother to participate as a result (even though they might be perfectly placed to supply the requirement). In February 2011, the Cabinet Office therefore introduced a mandatory PQQ form for all central government departments and their executive agencies (see the box below). All other contracting authorities are 'strongly encouraged' to use it as well.

In February 2011, a notice was published by the Cabinet Office to all central government departments including their executive agencies and non-departmental public bodies, mandating the use of a standard PQQ in the future for all above-threshold tenders. Furthermore, the notice stated that PQQs should not be used for below-threshold opportunities in the future. All other contracting authorities were 'strongly encouraged' to apply the requirements in the notice.

Regulation 23 criteria may still be applied in those ITTs issued without pre-qualification requirements, and financial checks can be undertaken to ensure that the supplier's financial position does not 'place public money or services at unacceptable risk'.

The standard PQQ can be viewed via the Cabinet Office website (see 'Electronic sources' in the References for the link). It contains a set of mandatory questions and allows for additional, discretionary questions to be asked.

Note: In the UK construction industry, a specially designed PQQ, known as PAS91, is used to pre-qualify potential suppliers. Designed by the British Standards Institution (BSI), it contains a core set of mandatory questions to test the suppliers' 'areas of capability'. In addition, project-specific questions are likely to be asked to further establish suitability. Further information is available from the BSI website (see 'Electronic sources' in the References for the link).

Clearing the PQQ hurdle

This can sometimes be much harder than you think. The PQQ process is designed to identify a manageable number of suppliers (normally between 4 and 10) who are deemed suitable to participate in the formal tendering process. There are often pass/fail criteria within the PQQ; the rest of the questions attract a score. These evaluation criteria should be made clear to you – if not, ask for them before you submit. You may or may not be told whether there's an overall passmark, or whether only the highest-scoring suppliers will pass through this stage. Again, it doesn't hurt to ask.

Information requested in a PQQ

To determine operational suitability, the buyer will construct a questionnaire that will typically request information about subjects such as trading history, experience in similar projects, organization structure and ownership, quality management, and health and safety management. Questionnaires often ask for information about insurance cover and contract disputes, and sometimes for references from existing customers. More recently, questions about environmental policies, sustainability and corporate social responsibility are being asked. They will also check that there are no legal reasons why you can't bid.

Of course, depending on the contract to be awarded, other relevant questions might also be included at this stage. You might also find that some seemingly irrelevant questions are asked too. This might be because the buying organization has a generic PQQ document that it sends out to all suppliers, regardless of the eventual requirement. In these instances, you'll still need to answer all the questions, however unnecessary you think they are.

Completing the PQQ

Look carefully, then, at the information requested, and be objective about how your answers look. If there are stated requirements that you can't meet (a particular safety certificate, say), it's unlikely that you'll make it through the first cut. Similarly, if you can't provide the required number of references or don't have the right experience to show, you are likely to be unsuccessful this time. An unconvincing approach to quality control, an over-reliance on subcontractors, or a newly established consortium might also weaken your appeal. It's a matter of using your common sense when completing a PQQ. This stage is about presenting facts, not spinning a good sales story.

Even if you're satisfied you have all the right credentials, don't fall down on a technicality. Be absolutely certain to answer every question meticulously.

If you're asked to tick a box to show you've attached your health and safety policy, make sure that you do both things (tick and attach!). It's not unusual for suppliers to be disqualified for such minor omissions.

Remember, any supplier can express an interest, so buyers often find that they have many more PQQs submitted than they have places on the short-list. Therefore, in much the same way that CVs are scanned and brutally discarded by HR departments, so are PQQ documents assessed by buyers. At this stage they're looking for reasons to disqualify, so will first set aside any questionnaires that are incomplete or incorrectly filled in.

Let's consider the key PQQ requirements in more detail.

Your legal position

Regulation 23 of the Public Contracts Regulations (as introduced in Chapter 2) sets out a number of grounds on which a bidder would be deemed 'ineligible to tender'.

There are some mandatory and some discretionary grounds for ineligibility. Normally, the PQQ will show the complete set of mandatory criteria, and those discretionary criteria that the buyer has chosen to include.

You will normally be asked to assert that you are not ineligible by answering a set of yes/no questions and then signing a declaration. Clearly, if any of the following apply to one or more directors of your organization, you are likely to be deemed ineligible and will not pass through the pre-qualification stage. If any one or more of them do apply, I would advise seeking legal advice prior to committing any further time to the completion of the PQQ.

Mandatory grounds for ineligibility are:

- conspiracy, in relation to participation in a criminal organization (as defined in the regulations);
- corruption (as defined);
- bribery;
- fraud (as defined);
- money laundering;
- other offences (as defined).

Discretionary grounds for ineligibility are:

- bankruptcy;
- conviction of a criminal offence in relation to business or professional conduct;

- non-payment of social security contributions or taxes;
- serious misrepresentation in this or other procurement processes;
- non-possession of the necessary licence, authorization or professional licence.

The only other legal position that might need to be clarified is that of the status of your organization. The buyer will need to be sure that you are a legally recognized entity; otherwise the buyer will not be able to contract with you in the event of your bid being successful. If you are creating a new company, charity or other legal body in order to bid, make sure all of your paperwork is in order before you submit your PQQ.

Your financial position

One of the key things the questionnaire will ask you about is your financial position over the past one to three years. You will need to provide evidence, in the form of audited accounts or a financial statement for each year. Let's explore the reason why this is so important to the buyer.

The buyer needs to be certain that your organization is sufficiently robust to fulfil the terms of the contract for its duration and will therefore wish to see information that will provide reassurance about your ongoing viability.

In the public sector especially, the value of the contract for which you are bidding versus your current turnover is an entry-level, pass/fail criterion that must be met to the buyer's satisfaction.

It's a simple calculation:

$$\frac{\text{Value of contract}}{\substack{\text{your current turnover (as shown in your} \\ \text{most recent annual accounts)}}} \times \substack{100 \text{ (to arrive at} \\ \text{a percentage result)}}$$

For example: if your turnover is currently £500,000, and the contract you are bidding for is valued at £400,000, or 80 per cent of your current revenue, the buyer would often perceive this as too risky. The actual ceiling limit on this will be determined in advance of the opportunity being advertised.

If your result is anything more than 25 per cent, it is well worth asking the buyer whether there is indeed a ceiling on this criterion. Be honest with the buyer about your position and ask if this might work against you in the evaluation process, or even exclude you totally.

You might not want to draw attention to this fact, but a good buyer will be happy to talk to you about this situation, especially if you can introduce the possibility of some form of guarantee to mitigate the risk.

Do I need to provide audited accounts?

Often, a PQQ will request that you submit your most recent *audited* accounts. The process of auditing is not the same as getting your accountant to process and finalize your books for you at the year-end; being audited requires you to go to the expense of appointing an independent auditor. However, in the UK, companies are exempted from needing to have their accounts audited if they have: a turnover of no more than £6.5 million; and a balance sheet total of no more than £3.26 million. (There are other cases in which an otherwise exempted company might need to proceed with an audit – where shareholders with more than a 10 per cent holding request it, for instance. It's best to seek clarification on this matter if any doubts exist in your own case.)

Therefore, if you see a request for audited accounts in a PQQ and you know you are exempt, state this clearly in your response. There is no need to go to the expense of appointing an auditor. Simply submit your (unaudited) accounts. I recommend the full rather than abbreviated version, since it contains all the information the buyer needs.

I sometimes wonder if buyers are simply using the wrong terminology when they ask for audited accounts, or perhaps they are not aware of the small business exemption. If there's any doubt, ask the question before you submit your response.

Insurance

As part of their checks on your suitability to supply, buyers will want assurance that your company is appropriately insured for the work you undertake on their behalf.

The main types of insurance you will be expected to provide are:

- employer's liability;
- public liability;
- product liability (for contracts under which you are supplying goods);
- professional indemnity (for service-based contracts).

The buyer will stipulate the level of cover required in the PQQ, which should be proportionate to the size of the contract. However, occasionally a standard document is used, or (perish the thought) the buyer cuts and pastes from a previous PQQ and leaves a higher-than-necessary minimum cover requirement figure in the text. If you feel that the level of cover is disproportionate to the specific contract to be provided, it's worth raising the matter with the buyer before the submission date. Doing so will often see the required level of cover amended.

Should I buy insurance cover (or increase my existing policy) during PQQ or ITT proceedings?

Until you are awarded a contract, there is technically no risk to insure, so it's common sense that you shouldn't have to have the stipulated level of insurance cover in place *until* the date on which the contract is signed. (Of course, by that time, the cover will be mandatory.) However, bidders are often unsure as to whether they should go ahead and get the new or increased cover stated in the PQQ or ITT.

My advice is this: 1) First check that your insurance company will insure to the level of risk required (and that you'd be happy to pay the premium, of course – this is part of your opportunity cost calculation; see Chapter 4). Ask them to provide a letter to you, confirming this. 2) Contact the buyer and clarify the situation, ensuring that the buyer will accept this 'letter of intent' in lieu of an actual certificate of cover during the bidding process. There's no reason that I can think of that would lead to the buyer rejecting this proposed course of action.

Policy documents

The buyer needs assurance that your company is well run and conducts its affairs effectively and ethically, and will therefore seek evidence of how things are managed on a day-to-day basis. This is why the buyer asks to see a variety of policies at the PQQ stage.

The most commonly requested policies at the PQQ stage are:

- anti-bribery;
- business continuity and disaster recovery (policy and plans);
- code of conduct;
- complaints;
- corporate social responsibility;
- customer care (including safeguarding, where appropriate);
- environmental (policy and method statement);
- equality and diversity;
- health and safety (policy and method statement);
- information security;
- lone working;
- quality management (policy and method statement);
- sustainability policy.

Of course, having a policy and actually implementing it are two quite different things. In some areas, therefore, you'll also be asked to provide evidence of your policies in action. This might be through reports or statistical evidence (the number of RIDDOR incidents within health and safety, for instance, or your carbon footprint for the previous year), or it might be in the form of a method statement. A method statement documents how you implement the policy in practice within your organization. It should detail specific actions taken, with measurable outcomes.

What to include in each policy could well form the subject of a whole book in itself. Regrettably, there simply isn't room here to cover all the possible elements you could include in each policy and method statement. However, there are plentiful resources available via the internet; sample policies abound. You can obtain free templates of most policies via this route; alternatively you'll find plenty of providers willing to sell them to you. As another option, you could always employ a specialist consultant to create a bespoke policy for you.

Whatever you do, though, never be tempted simply to admit that you don't have a policy, if one is requested (unless the requested policy could never possibly apply to your organization – which is not that likely). If necessary, work backwards from your day-to-day practice (or acknowledged best practice in your field), and incorporate these actions into a policy. But, if you are going to do this, ensure that you know whether there are legal considerations to be included in the policy (for instance, your anti-bribery policy must be written to align fully with the Bribery Act 2010, and your information security policy must align with the Data Protection Act).

I would caution that some aspects of your business will require specialist policy and method statement advice (health and safety being perhaps the most obvious). The content of others is purely down to you (corporate social responsibility, for instance).

Private sector shortlisting

As we have identified, private sector buyers are not encumbered by legislation that dictates how they select suppliers. As a result, as you'd expect, the way that tendering processes are run varies from buyer to buyer. If they are going to carry out any kind of pre-tendering suitability assessment, it is likely to be less formal than in the public sector.

The nearest comparable process to the public sector PQQ is the issuance of a request for information (RFI). Whilst this is not universally employed by buyers, if they are struggling to whittle down the number of potential bidders they might well ask you to complete one.

With a similar purpose to a PQQ, an RFI tries to identify your capability, capacity and experience to supply this opportunity. You could very well find yourself being required to provide information about how your business is structured, financed and governed. The type of information you are asked for is likely to be similar to that demanded by the public sector in a PQQ, as described above (accounts information, insurance, policies and the like). You might even find yourself having to provide indicative pricing at this stage.

The same rules apply to completing an RFI as apply to a PQQ. Provide a complete response to all the questions, and substantiate and provide evidence of your capability, experience and corporate governance. The buyer is looking to identify and disqualify risky-looking suppliers. Don't give buyers any reason not to include you at the next stage, when they issue the invitation to tender (ITT) or request for quote or proposal (RFQ or RFP).

SUMMARY

Take this stage seriously because, unless you successfully clear this hurdle, you won't be invited to bid. This is the part of the competition where the number of competitors is the highest, and buyers are looking for a way of bringing the numbers down. You've got to do all you can to ensure that you make it through.

It can be tough preparing for the pre-qualification stage. There's so much information to be gathered, and it can be disheartening in the early days. But, if you take a long-term view, not only will the next pre-qualification process be much quicker, but, away from the bidding, the information that you're gathering is useful for ensuring that your company is doing all the things it should do, well.

If you don't qualify, ask for feedback and identify the areas in which you failed or scored poorly compared to other bidders. Then take action to rectify the shortcomings, wherever possible, or recognize that future competitions might require improved or more robust credentials in order for you to compete.

Hopefully, though, you will make it through this stage and will be invited to participate in the next round of the competition. It's only then that you will have access to the detailed requirements and can begin to assess the opportunity for real.

The decision to bid

04

THIS CHAPTER COVERS:

- Factors that should affect your decision to bid
- Weighing it all up and making the big decision

It's a great feeling – maybe also a little daunting – when you've just found or have been sent an invitation to tender (ITT). You start to daydream about what it would be like to win this one: the new customer name on your website, the extra profit on the bottom line...

But let's not get ahead of ourselves here. Participating in a bid is a big deal – it can be a time-consuming, resource-hungry, costly process. You really need to be pretty certain that you've got a good chance of winning before you start spending time and money completing it. The best way to improve your win rate is to ensure that you have a robust 'decision to bid' process to follow. This will ensure that you go only for the right tenders and don't waste time on no-hopers.

Let's look at what that decision-making process looks like, then.

Factors that should affect your decision to bid

So, either you've made it through the pre-qualification or RFI process or, if you're lucky, you've received the ITT directly. But before you go any further or even think about bidding there are three big questions you need to ask yourself:

- Is it deliverable?

- Is it winnable?

- Will it be profitable?

It's got to be 'yes' for each one, as otherwise there really is no point in going to the effort of bidding. In this case, two out of three is just not good enough. Be honest with yourself, brutally so. At this stage, you've invested little, lost nothing. But make the wrong decision and, in a few weeks' time, the story could be very different. Take your time. This is an important decision.

Of course, underneath each of the three big questions are lots more that you'll need to ask yourself before you can finally arrive at the right answer. You'll have to weigh up the positives and the negatives for lots of factors before coming out with the right decision. To make this a little more scientific, it might be useful to create a simple scorecard to help with this, but we'll come to that in a little while.

First then, you need to start to identify your strengths, weaknesses, opportunities and threats. Start a SWOT diagram (as shown in Figure 4.1) to help you see the bigger picture and later to help you complete the scorecard. I promise this won't be wasted effort – if you decide to go ahead and bid, you'll find the SWOT to be a really valuable tool throughout the process.

FIGURE 4.1 SWOT diagram template

Strengths	Weaknesses
All the things that you will deliver well in this instance	All the things that you could improve in this instance
Opportunities	**Threats**
Things that you might be able to take advantage of to improve your chances of winning	Things that might happen to affect your proposed solution negatively

Let's now look at each big question in more detail to help you to populate the SWOT diagram.

Is it deliverable?

Too many companies give little thought to what it means to actually win a bid. I often hear the sentiment 'I'll worry about that later' or, if the person is in a larger organization, even worse, 'It won't be my problem by then'. If you're tempted to think like this, think again.

You need to make a more practical self-assessment about your ability to do the job from the first to the last day of the contract. You need to convince yourself or your team before you can even think about convincing a buyer! Let's break this down.

The basics

You need to be confident that you are aware of any risks that might get in the way of your successful delivery of the contract. You'll also need to have a plan for mitigating these. So start with the basics and then delve deeper:

- Have you done something similar before?
  - On this scale?
  - In this timeframe?
  - On this budget?
  - In this market?
- Do you have the resources to undertake the job?
  - Will you need new people, new skills, new equipment or new premises to do the job?
  - If so, how are you going to finance this development?
  - Will you have to subcontract any aspect of the work, hire in 'experts' at any stage or even find a partner organization to help deliver the contract?
  - If so, will this strengthen your proposition, or highlight the gap in your core capability to the buyer?
- What will be the impact on your other customers if you win this contract?
  - Will they experience a reduction in the quality of service they receive?
  - What might that mean in the long term?

Mark up your findings accordingly on the SWOT.

Showstoppers

There's often one requirement in a bid that you wish you could remove, because you just don't know how you're going to meet it. It's the gaping hole in your solution: the 'showstopper'. A showstopper might be: an unachievable service level with stringent penalties attached; an implementation schedule you can't meet; a guarantee you can't provide; terms and conditions in the agreement that you can't sign up to; a skill that you don't have; or functionality that your IT system can't deliver.

However tempting it is to ignore a showstopper, please don't. Address it here and now. Put it in capital letters as a threat on your SWOT, and don't do anything else until you've solved this one.

Don't despair at this stage, though. Often your showstopper is every other bidder's too. Establish this fact, if you can. If necessary, talk to the buyer about just how important this element is overall, so that you can put it into perspective.

If, after careful consideration, you still can't solve the problem, it's probably best to decide against bidding this time.

If you think you've solved the problem, great. This threat has now become a strength. If this was a showstopper that you believed other bidders would be struggling to solve, does this now give you a differentiator to sell? Update your SWOT and move on to the next big question.

Is it winnable?

Before you start to work on this question, imagine you're preparing a two-minute pitch for a *Dragons' Den*-style panel. Could you really convince them that the investment needed to pursue this opportunity would give a definite financial return? (Remember, time is money, so, even if you don't need to make any capital investment, can you afford to waste the time?) Better still, actually present the pitch to colleagues, investors or stakeholders – or even, if you're a one-person outfit, to a friend or your better half. Does it still sound convincing when you 'sell' it to someone else? Take onboard any feedback you get and adapt accordingly.

To really make your pitch watertight, you'll need to consider a number of factors, covered in more detail below. Plot your findings for each on your SWOT.

Incumbency

If you are the incumbent (existing supplier), great! You should have an advantage, provided you've been doing a good job up until now. Put this as a strength on the SWOT. (If your relationship isn't as good as it could be, put it as a weakness, have a look at Chapter 8 for further advice and then come back to this question!) Of course, buyers are always looking to reduce costs, so as the incumbent you might have to prepare to add extra value or reduce your price.

But you know the culture of the organization, understand its vision and strategy, know the people and anticipate what's expected. In addition, they know you and what you can do; they know your people and your (collective) attitude. It's a great starting position.

However, don't be complacent! Other bidders will be looking to persuade the buyer to switch away from you and will put up a case for change. You'll need to make sure you tell the opposite story: telling the buyer why continuity will be the best approach. Often, as the incumbent, you have to work that little bit harder than other bidders, to show how much more you know and how much more you want the contract than they do. Make sure you're prepared for this extra effort.

If you're not the incumbent, the first thing I recommend you do is try to find out if there is one. If this is a public sector contract, this is a little bit easier, as the information is in the public domain. If it's a private sector contract, it's still possible to find out – the first place to look is on your competitors' websites for case studies. (It's amazing how much information is given away via PR.) But really, the easiest way to find out is to ask the buyer. Buyers might not tell you who the incumbent is, but they should tell you if there is one.

So let's say there's an incumbent. Try to think of anything specific that you'd need to match or overcome to beat them. You'll need to find out a little bit about them (go back to the internet for a look at their website, or use other research channels, if you don't already know them well) to work out what your strengths and weaknesses are, relative to theirs.

Next, take a close look at the tender document, at the information given to bidders. Does it seem to favour the incumbent? Look for these kinds of clues:

- You don't seem to have been given all the information you need to create a full solution.
- There are some impossible conditions that only the incumbent could meet (location, experience, software, etc).
- The submission deadline is even shorter than normal.
- It doesn't ask for information on how you would manage the migration of the contract from the existing supplier to the new supplier.

- It's a public sector contract and all the contract extension options have been taken up previously, so it has to go back out to open competition now. (This doesn't mean it has to be awarded to a new supplier, though, just that the buyer is required to ensure that the 'most economically advantageous tender' is selected. This could easily be the incumbent's.)

One of the most telling things of all, though, is the buyer's attitude to your requests for information. It's a buyer's job to get the best solution at the best price. So it's in buyers' interest to give you the information you need to prepare your best bid. If they don't seem that interested in helping you get to that place, there's probably a good reason. Maybe they've already made their decision and don't need to waste time engaging with the market. If you come across a buyer who is reluctant to talk, make a note of this on the SWOT, accordingly.

Once you've done all this research, chart what you know about the incumbent on the SWOT. The more embedded the incumbent looks, the bigger the threat! On the other hand, if it looks as though the buyer wants to move away from a poorly performing incumbent, this could be an excellent opportunity.

There's one more possible scenario with regard to an incumbent – there isn't one. This could be because this is a brand new requirement or because the previous supplier hasn't been invited to rebid, their contract was terminated or they went out of business. Either way this is good news for you, but also for your competitors. It does mean that the playing field is a little more level, but it also means that any threats that are out there are less visible to you. If you feel you've got a good handle on the marketplace and your competitors and that you have a differentiator that will give you the edge, put this as a strength on your SWOT.

How you came about the opportunity

There are many ways an opportunity will come to your attention: perhaps through a public register, straight from the customer or via a consultant, newspaper advert or your local chamber of commerce. Of course, there are many more. Clearly, some of these routes will be more favourable to you than others.

Getting to know a prospective customer before they put an opportunity out to the market is clearly advantageous. The more people you know in that organization, and the better understanding you have of their vision, values and challenges, the better placed you will be in any bidding situation.

At the point at which they have an opportunity to send out to the market, you'll be on the distribution list. Even better, they might approach you first or ask your advice on putting the ITT together. You're in pole position when this happens – a definite strength on the SWOT.

If you've picked up an opportunity from a public register, there are likely to be many others doing the same. What differentiator(s) do you believe you have that will set you apart from all of these other bidders? Why will they pick your solution over everyone else's? Just bear in mind the fact that you are much less likely to win a bid 'from cold', and mark it as a threat on the SWOT. You'll really need to stand out from the pack during the bid evaluation stage to overcome this one.

Your financial position

In Chapter 3 we looked at how buyers request financial information as part of any pre-qualification stage to assess your likely financial security throughout the contract term. They want to be certain that you'll be able to meet your obligations from start to finish. If you haven't had to provide financial information before now, and it's a requirement of your bid submission, take an objective look at your situation. (You might find it useful to look back at the PQQ section in Chapter 3 to see how to do this.)

Don't ignore this issue and hope that your submission will 'wow' the buyer sufficiently to take a risk on you. Save yourself huge amounts of time and effort by establishing the buyer's attitude to this risk right at the outset of the process.

Decide whether your financial position is a strength or a weakness (from the buyer's perspective, that is). Then mark it up on your SWOT accordingly.

Experience

One of your best selling tools is the experience and expertise you can show to prospective customers from past projects and contracts that your organization has worked on. Being able to point to such experience changes a bid from a claim of competence to a statement of demonstrable ability. Buyers always want to avoid risk, and will look for reassurance that your bid does not contain anything that might put the project in any kind of jeopardy.

Think about the experience that you can show to the buyer for this opportunity. Will you be able to convince the buyer that you've done this kind of thing before? It doesn't even matter if you haven't carried out one single similar project that ticks all the boxes. Being able to demonstrate experience of individual elements across a range of customers is just as good – it shows your adaptability. A range of case studies and a team of people with their own 'back stories' to draw upon should definitely go on to your SWOT as a strength.

Conversely, if you've no experience at all in delivering the kind of service that the customer needs, this is definitely a weakness on your SWOT. If you were choosing builders to build an extension on your house and they couldn't show you any photos of completed jobs or provide any references, would you take them on? Doubtful. Why would professional buyers take a gamble on inexperience when it's their reputation on the line?

References

There's nothing better to further reassure a buyer of your competence than a set of references from happy customers with whom you've previously worked (or are currently working).

You'll often be asked to provide references as part of the bidding process, so think early on about who would give you the most relevant reference. Ideally, you would match references to the case studies you're going to include in the bid. Are you still in touch with the right contacts, and could you approach them to obtain their permission to be named as references in your bid?

If you're confident about the quality, strength and relevance of your references, put this as a strength on your SWOT. Otherwise, it's a weakness, I'm afraid, and something you'll need to work on in time for your next bid.

Time and resource to bid

Remember this is a competition. You need to be better than everyone else. You need to draw the best possible solution out of your team. You need to be creative, innovative, eye-catching and thought-provoking. To draw up the best submission you need time to think.

Have a look at the task ahead of you and try to estimate how long it would take to prepare a winning bid – not just a compliant bid (have a look ahead at Chapter 6 to see what this entails). I accept this as a near-impossible task (I hate doing it myself, and I've written more bids than I care to remember), but you need to have an idea of what you're committing to. Now add on at least 25 per cent more time than you initially envisaged. Trust me, these things take so much longer than you ever want them to.

Once you've an idea how long it's going to take, think about who's actually going to do the work. It's likely that you'll need to consult with other people, some internal, possibly some external. How challenging will it be to get their time and attention? What about geographical challenges – if all the people you'll need are on the road, or on holiday, or based in other offices, or tied up with existing projects, how are you going to manage this 'virtual' team? If pertinent, the potential loss of focus on existing projects is a threat and should be marked as such on your SWOT.

At this point, do a quick calculation about how much this bid is going to cost you to submit, using the following calculation:

Number of hours × an estimated cost per hour
+ bid production and delivery costs
+ expenses (travel, research, samples, etc)

A back-of-an-envelope calculation will do for now (really, it doesn't need to be more than that). But it will reveal to you the investment you'll be making in this bid. It's always quite sobering to realize just how much, win or lose, you will be spending on this process.

Put the investment figure as a threat on your SWOT (on the grounds that this is what you stand to lose). You'll also need this number to answer the 'Profitable?' question.

Finally, armed with the knowledge that you're going to be spending time and money, and it's an all-or-nothing job, can you afford to go for it? (Or, depending on your circumstances, can you afford not to?) There's no magic formula for making this call, but at least you'll know what you're letting yourself in for if you do decide to go ahead.

Other competitors' strengths and weaknesses

We've already considered the challenges associated with bidding against an incumbent, but in most competitions there'll be other bidders to consider too. Hopefully, you'll be aware of your competition and will have a good idea who else might be considering bidding for this opportunity. Even if you don't have a distinct idea of the actual companies, you'll know what the marketplace is currently offering.

This is a really important part of your decision to bid – because you need to start thinking about what you can offer the buyer that no one else can. This is your differentiator.

Differentiators are sometimes difficult to pin down. Some obvious examples are price, experience, quality, your people and their experience, your location/proximity to the customer, cultural fit or your charging mechanism. There can be many more, but you need to be clear in your own mind about what you're offering versus everyone else. This one factor will become central to your bid, so think hard and be honest with yourself. What are you offering that's truly different? Will any other bidder be able to claim the same differentiator? If so, it's back to the drawing board, I'm afraid – this is a benefit, but not a differentiator. (If you need more help on benefits and differentiators, have a look at Chapter 6.)

Buyers need to justify to themselves and to the ultimate decision makers that they are making the right recommendation. Having a clear differentiator makes this so much easier for them. Often, buyers have no choice but to revert to the differentiator that is easiest to identify – price. If you have a clear proposition that demonstrates the added value that you can offer, you can avoid this scenario.

Having a clear and valuable differentiator is a mega-strength. Mark it up on your SWOT in capital letters!

Cultural fit

Buyers need to be reassured that their supplier will understand what is required and will work within what are often unspoken boundaries. Have a look at the customer's culture. Are they leading-edge, innovative, pioneering, early adopters in their field? Then they're likely to want suppliers whose energy and creativity can keep pace with their own. Conversely, if their reputation is for safe, controlled, risk-free services, they are likely to want a supplier that is focused on process, trust and solid, proven techniques.

Although you'll always have to adapt your story to fit the customer's requirements, make sure you would be happy working within their boundaries. Would this way of working suit your company's style and allow you to do the best job? It has to work both ways.

Take a step back and look at how your SWOT is shaping up. How does it look so far? More strengths than weaknesses? Great. You can always address your weaknesses. The incumbent as the main threat? Not the end of the world. A clear differentiator? Fantastic. Extra opportunities to sell additional services or add value? Excellent. So far so good, but it's now time to look at what it would mean to your bottom line if you won the bid.

Will it be profitable?

Clearly, you don't want to lose money if you're awarded this contract. You'll therefore need to have all the financial facts at your fingertips in order to make the right decision on this opportunity.

This particular question is one that you'll need to keep coming back to during the course of your bid, because things will almost always change as you put your solution together. You'll need to keep reassuring yourself that the answer is still 'yes', on balance. For now, you're establishing whether or not you can afford to put forward a competitive bid and still make money.

Price up the delivery of the job, as you would normally. Estimate at this stage; remember you're trying to establish whether you want to commit to bidding; you're not actually working on the bid yet. (Don't worry, though – all this preparation will be used if you do decide to go ahead.) Then think about the following factors.

Opportunity-specific costs

On top of your normal cost model, which will already account for known, day-to-day operating costs, your considerations should include additional, opportunity-specific costs. Be really careful that you think of every possibility; it's very easy for your future profit to be eroded by unanticipated costs such as recruitment fees.

Opportunity-specific costs might include:

- bid resource costs (you hopefully did a quick calculation of this when you were considering the 'winnable' question);
- tooling or sample creation costs;
- the cost of checking your prospect's financial position or other research you might need to buy;
- set-up, transition and close-down costs;
- costs for buying in or recruiting additional expertise or resource;
- training and development costs;
- service penalties;
- increased insurance premiums for additional cover required by the customer;
- costs associated with providing any financial guarantees.

I would always recommend including a contingency element in your calculations, appropriate to the risks inherent in your solution, to cover any unforeseen elements that might later arise.

Once you have a view of your overall costs, you will then need to consider the price you will charge the customer in this instance. In some cases, the buyer will include a budget figure in the tender document to help you to see if you're on the right lines.

You'll also need to consider cash flow: when and how will you invoice the customer and what are their payment terms? How will set-up costs be treated?

You now need to take the contract term into consideration, so that you can calculate your break-even point across the contract lifetime. This is a key factor in your decision.

Finally, look at the business case that you've now created for this opportunity. You've got most of the information you need to make your decision about profitability, but there are two more very important considerations to be made yet.

1. The customer's financial position

It's often overlooked in the excitement of the opportunity, but your revenue and indeed your profit are all theoretical until you actually get paid. You'll need, therefore, to be as certain as you can be that this customer is in a strong enough financial position now, and for the duration of the contract, to pay you for the goods and services that you provide. This is especially important if there are steep set-up costs that the customer requests to spread out over the contract lifetime, or if your break-even point comes late in the contract term.

There are a number of companies from which you can obtain credit risk information for a relatively small fee. I recommend taking this option; it'll be a worthwhile investment in the long run.

The most risky contracts are those being awarded by start-ups, since you won't have any historical information to draw upon. Proceed with caution here.

In a similar vein, if the tender is being managed by consultants and they are not willing to tell you who the customer is at this stage, be cautious. Try to find out why they won't disclose. Until you know who your customer is, consider this a definite threat and mark it on the SWOT as such. Come back to this consideration as soon as you know who the customer is, and reposition this on the SWOT accordingly.

Clearly, public sector contracts are free from the risk of insolvency or cash flow problems, but there are other potential risks in supplying to a public sector body, and we'll explore these next.

2. External factors that might affect the contract

For the majority of contracts requiring ongoing services or repeat orders for goods, suppliers are expected to accommodate a good degree of the risk inherent within them. Try to identify any external risks that might interfere with the customer's ongoing need for the goods and services you're contracted to supply, and then consider how probable these risks seem over the contract term.

In both the public and the private sector, I have seen service-based contracts that don't meet the volume or activity projections included in the original

ITT, so projected revenues never materialize as a result. (In most cases, the contracts are weighted with the risk being at the supply end.) Similarly, in goods-based contracts, I've seen end-user demand that doesn't meet sales projections result in orders being trimmed right back.

Public sector contracts are often seen as the holy grail for suppliers, and many a sales director dreams of landing that elusive first publicly funded contract. In many ways that's true, but just be aware that things might not always be quite as certain as you first perceive them to be. I've seen changes of government, or policy, or legislation negate the need for a supplier almost overnight. In these cases, the supplier has no say in such matters, and contracts don't protect them from these decisions. In fact there are normally clauses in public sector contracts that cover such eventualities; suppliers are not likely to receive compensation in these cases.

Have a good think about any factors that might scupper your revenue and profit projections. The weather; the fickle nature of consumers or end-users; industrial action: all out of your control, but all potentially your headache. If any of them are more likely to happen than not (your call, I'm afraid!), mark them up on your SWOT as a threat.

Weighing it all up and making the big decision

You're now ready to weigh up the good things (strengths and opportunities on the left of your SWOT) against the bad things (weaknesses and threats on the right) in order to make your decision. If you can see at a glance that your SWOT is heavily weighted towards the right half of your SWOT, this might be enough for you to view the decision as a no-brainer.

But, as is normally the case, it's just not that easy to call. You might need to use a simple scorecard to be absolutely certain where the balance point lies. Don't worry, this is pretty straightforward to manage.

Your scorecard just needs to have three columns (deliverable, winnable, profitable). Each item on your SWOT will be given a mark on the scorecard under the relevant column. Record your strengths and opportunities under the relevant column with a positive number (say +5 or +10, depending on how good they are). Record your weaknesses and threats with a negative number (say –5 or –10, depending on how bad they are). You'll have to use your judgement here, but be realistic about the scores you give! When you've allocated a score to each item, calculate the total for each column.

Two examples of completed scorecards are shown in Tables 4.1 and 4.2.

TABLE 4.1   Sample scorecard 1

Deliverable	Winnable	Profitable
Have sufficient capacity: +5	New contract (no incumbent), plus worked successfully with this customer previously: +5	High-margin product: +10
Would need to bring in extra staff: –5	Invited to tender by the buyer: +5	Will have to absorb training costs for new staff: –5
Have required safety certification: +5	Strong financial position: +5	Competitors will offer discounted rates to win the business: –5
Could begin within required timeframe: +5	Lots of similar experience with other customers and good references available: +5	Customer is a public body; no risk of non-payment: +5
Will need to subcontract one step of the solution, but will use proven partner: 0	The person who was going to write the bid is on holiday: –5	No known risk factors that might affect demand: 0
Have unique approach that will improve quality for no additional cost (differentiator): +10	Competitors can offer similar solution: –5	Set-up costs can be charged within first 12 months: +5
	Good cultural fit: +5	
Total score: +20	**Total score: +15**	**Total score: +10**

TABLE 4.2 Sample scorecard 2

Deliverable	Winnable	Profitable
Would have to bring in external expert to fill knowledge gap for key role: −5	No incumbent – brand new requirement: +5	High-value service, good profit potential: +10
Project clashes with another customer's and quality might be compromised: −5	Picked up the tender from the chamber of commerce register; open competition, no relationship with buyer: −5	Will be able to fully on-charge costs for the external expert: +5
Have required quality system in place: +5	Able to provide all financial reports required and contract would account for less than 5 per cent of turnover: +5	Customer is a start-up with no financial history; presents cash flow risk: −10
Could not begin within required timeframe: −5	Only partial experience of similar activities with other customers: −5	Attractive bonus offered for overperformance: +5
No need to subcontract any part of the solution: 0	Limited bid resource available: −5	Demand for the required service is uncertain; presents income risk: −5
	Competitors would also struggle to show experience: +5	
	Don't know much about the customer's vision, culture or values (start-up): −5	
Total score: −10	**Total score: −5**	**Total score: +5**

When your totals are recorded, take a good look. If your scorecard is negative in any column, or if one column is significantly lower than the others, this should really challenge your thinking.

A low relative score for 'deliverable' might mean that you'd never score enough points in the evaluation to convince the buyer that you could do the job. Or worse, you might win the contract and then be stuck trying to invest unplanned time, resource or capital in meeting your obligations.

If it doesn't score well under 'winnable', even if it does under 'deliverable' and 'profitable', then this opportunity is more appealing to you than you are to its buyer!

If you win it and can deliver it, but it's not profitable, would you want it on your books?

Using the two sample scorecards, then, what would be the right decision?

- Scorecard 1: Positive score against each big question, good balance, no showstoppers. Bid!
- Scorecard 2: Two negative scores, skew towards profitable, lots of potential risks. Don't bid.

So the three big questions have been considered; let's hope you've decided that the answer is a resounding 'yes' to each of them. That's fantastic. (You didn't engineer things to arrive at the outcome you wanted all along, did you?) You must be brutally honest with yourself when making this call – there's a lot of work ahead and plenty at stake...

If you're going ahead, you now have a completed SWOT, which will be a really important tool during the rest of the process. Stick it up where you can see it, and send a copy round to everyone who'll be contributing to the bid – they'll all need to know what's in store. And get ready for the next stage: the bid itself.

If you decided not to go ahead, commiserations. At least you can satisfy yourself that you made a good decision, not based on gut feel but on a well-constructed business case. You've probably learnt a lot about your organization in going through this decision-making process. Make sure that you use any lessons that you have learnt to get ready for the next opportunity. You'll be in much better shape when it does arrive.

...And keep making it

I'm afraid the decision to bid isn't a once-only step in the whole process, but is one that you should continually make as you work your way through towards the deadline.

Often something will happen during the course of your preparations that will call your original decision into question. This might be a change in requirement from the customer, or a discovery about a competitor's situation, or a realization that your solution suddenly costs too much. The buyer might move the deadline or stipulate a new instruction (buyer's prerogative, I'm afraid), or your legal adviser might counsel you against accepting the terms of the contract. It could be anything, really, and you'll know, when it arrives, that it can't be ignored. So go with that instinct, don't ignore it, keep your SWOT and scorecard up to date and cut your losses, if necessary.

It takes so much more courage to stop a bid than to carry on with it; I know this from personal experience. I have worked on several bids where something happened part-way through that made it suddenly undeliverable, unwinnable or unprofitable. Of course, having started the process in complete favour of proceeding, it can be very difficult to admit to yourself, let alone persuade your team, just why you're changing your mind so completely now. But this is where your scorecard and SWOT come in; you can show the team the criteria that you've been balancing all along and what has changed to tip that balance.

If you do decide to withdraw, make sure you notify the buyer as soon as you can. In some cases, the buyer will try to dissuade you from pulling out (but, remember, it's in their interest to keep as many bidders in the process as is possible) and will probably want to know why you're not going to submit, so be prepared to discuss your reasons with them.

Don't be despondent after you've pulled out of the competition; call a meeting for your contributors, have a discussion about what you've all learnt and put that learning into practice next time you bid. Celebrate the fact that you've made a good call, and move on. Hopefully there'll be plenty of new (deliverable, winnable and profitable) opportunities just around the corner.

SUMMARY

Never proceed with a bid before you've asked yourself the three big questions: deliverable, winnable, profitable? Take time to consider the case for bidding; draw up a SWOT and outline your solution costs. I promise you that it'll be time well spent.

Once you've decided to bid, keep checking it's still a good decision; don't be afraid to pull out of the competition if something fundamental changes.

Keeping on track

05

Where to start and how to finish

THIS CHAPTER COVERS:

- Getting started on your bid
- Project-managing your bid
- Formatting and populating the document
- Submitting on time

By now, you've made the decision to bid, and you've sketched out a SWOT. You're keen to get going, to start writing, to feel like you're doing something to get you advanced towards a finished document. This chapter will guide you through the process of constructing your bid from start to finish and will help you to avoid panics and disasters along the way. But we're not going to think about writing anything just yet. This chapter covers how to manage your time and resources; we'll start thinking about what to write in Chapter 6.

Some of the tools and techniques I describe here may be overkill for the bid that you're working on and you may not need them all every time. That said, the majority of these steps are must-do activities that you should always complete, regardless of the size of the opportunity or the perceived complexity of the tender document from the customer. Skimp on them at your peril!

Getting started on your bid

Before you start, decide how you're going to tackle the task ahead and then plan accordingly. As clichéd as it may be, time is money. Whilst you don't want to waste time, equally a half-hearted job will not win the bid.

Step 1 – read and reread the customer's document (must-do)

This sounds a bit obvious, doesn't it? But I know how these things often play out; you skim-read the customer's document (PQQ, ITT, RFP, etc) when it first arrived (be honest, you didn't read every word, did you?) and now you're itching to get going and you think you have a pretty good idea of what's required... that'll do, won't it?

If that sounds familiar, we'll now explore why 'pretty good' is not good enough and how you need to read everything at least twice.

The first read-through

Read the ITT (let's refer to it as that in this chapter, even though it might well be an RFP, RFI, RFQ, etc) slowly and completely, making notes and highlighting important instructions.

After this first read-through, complete a quick checklist:

1 Do you have all the information you need to start preparing your bid, or are there any pieces of missing information or ambiguities in the document? Do you have any doubts at all about what's required? Start preparing a list of questions for the buyer.

2 Are there any specific instructions that you're going to need to prepare for? For instance, do you need to obtain references, print and bind several hard copies, book a courier or attach copies of your latest accounts? Some of these things may take a while to organize, so think about them early on.

3 Do you have access to all the right people in your organization during the bid period? Now you're getting into the detail of preparing to bid, make sure you can assemble the right team and that they can all commit the time and effort required.

The second read-through

Now, you need to read the customer's document again, this time reading between the lines. You're trying to identify the things that are implied in the requirements but are not explicitly requested. This is a really important stage of the process, because it's the first stage in ensuring that your bid submission is truly customer-focused.

Your research into the customer or discussions with them might have revealed the most important factors in their day-to-day operations. Their statement of values (often published on their website) may reinforce the importance of these factors, as may their annual report. Recent news stories about them may identify a particular challenge that needs to be overcome or a particular area of emphasis that they promote. In the tender documents, these factors or challenges may not be listed as primary requirements.

You might also notice that there are questions about certain topics in the document that attract a higher score than others. For example, perhaps the buyer is particularly concerned about information security, or transition risk (moving from the old supplier to a new one), or environmental impact, etc, and has included specific questions to assess your capability to manage these.

All of these 'hidden' requirements are often ones that you can use to elevate your bid from a compliant one (that meets all the explicit requirements) to a winning one (that meets all the unwritten ones as well). So your second read-through is just as important as the first.

Keep looking for these unwritten or unspoken requirements during your everyday interactions with the customer (if you already have a relationship) and throughout the bid preparation. They could make the difference between winning and losing.

Project-managing your bid

Step 2 – prepare a bid timetable (must-do)

This doesn't need to be a detailed, complex document, I promise you. This part of the process just needs a common-sense approach to time management and good discipline to make it happen. However you decide to go about it, you must set a timetable, share it with anyone else who's involved in the bid and then stick to it!

If you're looking for help on how to schedule the bid, here's the way I normally start planning.

Add in your milestones and tasks/events

Initially, there will be only two dates in your timetable: receipt date (day you received the ITT from the customer); and deadline date. Draw up a table, showing these milestones in the first and final rows respectively.

Now calculate how much time you have between the two dates. If you're lucky (and/or organized), this will be in days; add in and label up a corresponding number of rows on your table. Blank out weekends (unless you or the team are prepared to work them) and any other unavailable time you know about already.

By now, a clear picture of how much time you've really got for this bid will be emerging.

Next, you need to add in other key tasks and events, each on a new row, against the date on which it needs to be completed. To do this, work backwards. Start at the deadline date, and work out what will need to be done, in reverse order, until you get back to today's date.

On your first bid, you'll probably be a bit stumped as to what you need to include in your timetable. Clearly, there are many variables that will affect this, and every bid is different, so it's not possible to draw up a standard template that you can use. However, below is a list of the types of activities you might well need to include. If you're not sure what they are, they will be covered in more detail later. Read ahead if you need to, and come back to the timetable once you have a clearer idea of what needs to be done.

I've put them loosely in the order in which you'd need to carry them out, and have shown key milestones in bold text to give an indication of where they might come in the process:

Receipt date (day one)
Distribute ITT to contributors to read and to identify questions/missing information
Invite all contributors to kick-off meeting

Kick-off meeting
Agree high-level solution, bid theme and sales messages, including differentiators (at kick-off meeting)
Prepare outputs matrix and content checklist and distribute to all contributors (see below)
Draft the executive summary
Submit questions to buyer
Collect up solution costs
Prepare response template
Prepare content (as per the outputs matrix and the content checklist)
Draft pricing proposal

Mid-point review
Coach contributors on content improvements/changes arising
    from mid-point review
Receive final versions of content from contributors
Agree final pricing proposal
Add content into response template
Complete executive summary

Final review
Amendments to content and pricing after final review
Final proofread and check
Print production
Delivery

Deadline date (final day)

Add in deadlines

Now you need to allocate an appropriate amount of time to each task or event. Each needs to have its own deadline, based on the owner's availability, the length and complexity of the task and the output the owner needs to prepare. You will doubtless find that it's difficult to fit everything on to your timetable, so you'll need to jiggle things around to fit. Avoid, however, the mistake of making the task fit into the time available. If it needs three days, but you've only got space for one day in the schedule, stop and think. Go back to the 'deliverable' and 'winnable' questions again (from Chapter 4). If this lack of time compromises the potential quality of the bid submission, should you continue to work on it?

When adding tasks to your timetable, choose carefully, making sure you don't try to save time by missing anything out that might compromise the quality of the final submission. Remember, you need to submit a winning bid, not simply a compliant one.

Recognize that some tasks can be carried out in parallel. If they're not interdependent and don't have the same owners, you can plan for them to be done at the same time.

Be sure to build in review time; with the best will in the world, some of the work your contributors submit for inclusion in the document will need to be added to or rewritten. You need to accommodate this probable extra work in your scheduling.

Don't underestimate the time it takes to cut and paste together all the submissions that you receive into a single document. This can be quite a frustrating process, so leave plenty of time for it in your timetable.

Similarly, if your document needs to be printed and bound, be sure to allocate enough time to get this done. If you're going to produce it in-house, make sure that you factor in enough time for the inevitable paper jams, toner meltdowns, binder breakdowns and other general frustrations involved in producing your own documents. If you're going to an external printer's, make sure you're clear how much time they need to complete your job.

Always include at least 10 per cent contingency towards the end of your timetable (after your final review session). Something is bound to happen to mess up even the most thoughtfully constructed timetable. And if a miracle occurs and all goes smoothly, even better – you can use the time for an extra-detailed review.

Add in owners

Now add in a new column alongside each task/event and allocate it an owner. Make sure you only ever allocate one owner for each task to ensure there is no confusion about shared responsibility.

Finalize

By now, your timetable will be taking shape nicely, so the next task is to share it with your fellow bid contributors.

Figure 5.1 shows a simplified version of a timetable, to give you an idea of how it might look at this stage in your preparation.

Make sure contributors each acknowledge the tasks allocated to them and accept the deadlines allocated. Remind them that there is very little margin for error in the timetable, and ask them to formally schedule their own preparation time into their diaries.

Professional nagging – making sure everyone sticks to the schedule

One crucial piece of advice about your timetable: stick it up somewhere so that you can see it throughout the process, and encourage everyone else involved in the bid to look at it every day. If you work in a small office, stick up a large version where all your contributors can see it, and have a daily huddle around it to see what's on the list for that day.

It's vital that everyone takes the timetable seriously and that they know that you take it seriously too. Talk to task/event owners a day or so before their deadline(s) and ask how they're getting on. Coach them through their

FIGURE 5.1 Sample bid timetable

Bid timetable.xls

	Date	Event	Owner	Progress	Comments
	Monday 1st January	Receive ITT document	Bid Manager	Complete	Sent by e-mail with invitation to kick-off meeting
		Distribute document to bid team	Bid Manager	Complete	
	Tuesday 2nd January	Kick-off meeting	Bid Manager	Pending	
		Prepare and distribute work package matrix	Bid Manager	Pending	
		Submit questions to buyer	Bid Manager	Pending	
	Wednesday 3rd January	Draft Executive Summary	Sales Manager	Pending	
				Pending	
	Thursday 4th January	Prepare response template	Bid Manager	Pending	
	Friday 5th January	All solution costs collected and with Finance Manager	Finance Manager	Pending	
		First drafts of content sent to Bid Manager	Subject matter experts	Pending	
	Saturday 6th January				
	Sunday 7th January				
	Monday 8th January	Mid-point review meeting	All	Pending	
		Review draft pricing proposal	All	Pending	
	Tuesday 9th January	Final versions of content sent to Bid Manager	Subject matter experts	Pending	
	Wednesday 10th January	Final version of pricing proposal agreed	Finance Manager	Pending	
		Final version of Executive Summary completed	Sales Manager	Pending	
		All content edited and inserted into response template	Bid Manager	Pending	
	Tuesday 11th January	Final review meeting	All	Pending	
		Amendments and final proofread	Bid Manager	Pending	
	Friday 12th January	Contingency – morning	Bid Manager	Pending	
		Submit bid by e-mail before 16:00	Bid Manager	Pending	

Sheet1 Sheet2 Sheet3

tasks if they're struggling. But don't just cross your fingers and hope for the best.

I often describe my role in this part of the bid as 'professional nagging'. Anyone who's worked on a bid with me will be nodding vigorously at this point. But it's a very necessary part of the process and, as deadline day approaches, you'll be glad you made the effort.

As a bid manager, you need to manage your timetable actively; otherwise I can almost guarantee that you'll be trying to make up the lost ground yourself (unnecessary), working late in the few days before the bid (avoidable) or missing the deadline altogether (disastrous).

So hone your professional nagging skills, keep on top of your timetable, add in new things as they arise and tick tasks off as you successfully complete them. Do these things, and all will be well come deadline day.

Step 3 – prepare an outputs matrix (must-do)

An outputs matrix simply details all the individual outputs that need to be created in order to complete the bid. It is unlikely that these will all be listed in detail in the timetable, so you need a document that ensures you don't miss anything out accidentally when compiling the final submission.

That said, your outputs matrix should complement your timetable, and the two documents can even be combined if your bid is not too complicated – this is your call.

To begin populating your outputs matrix you'll need to go through the document and identify all the things you've been asked to provide in your response. The problem is, they're not always neatly in one place in the tender document. So, whilst you might have a list of questions to answer (easy to spot!), the buyer might also state, elsewhere in the document, that you should provide references, or annual accounts, or a statement of acceptance of standard terms and conditions, or the like. But these might be dotted around, or even mentioned in the covering letter rather than the main document. Look carefully!

When you're confident you've found everything you need to include in your response, these things need to go into your outputs matrix.

To be really clear, the kinds of things you need to include in your outputs matrix are:

- covering letter;
- executive summary (whether you are asked for one or not – more on this later);

- individual questions from the customer's tender document (you might want to cut and paste the text of the question itself so that there's no need to cross-refer back to the tender document);

- pricing proposal;

- statement about acceptance of terms and conditions or required amendments;

- references;

- case studies;

- annual accounts;

- biographies of key people;

- freedom of information statement (public sector bids only), in which you indicate if there are any parts of your bid that you wish not to be disclosed under the Freedom of Information Act;

- statement of non-collusion (often required in public sector bids).

This is by no means an exhaustive list. Each bid will have its own requirements; be sure you are clear what they all are from the outset.

As in the timetable, make sure that owners and deadlines are clearly shown.

An example of an outputs matrix is shown in Figure 5.2.

Helping contributors to manage multiple outputs

If any of your contributors have multiple outputs within the outputs matrix, consider giving them different deadlines for each output rather than asking them to submit everything to you on one day. In that way, they'll view the workload as a series of smaller tasks and won't feel overwhelmed by the overall volume (in theory, anyway!).

In addition, you get a chance to see how their work is shaping up during the course of the bid rather than in one go towards the end. This gives you a chance to coach them if early responses aren't quite up to scratch, and to request rewrites or additional input. It also makes life easier for you as you construct the document, avoiding the scenario where you're trying to populate your response template right at the end, as the deadline looms.

FIGURE 5.2 Sample outputs matrix

Outputs matrix.xls

	Item reference	Item	Section name	Question reference	Score or number of points allocated to this question	Owner	Internal deadline for submission to Bid Manager	Received? Yes/No	Comments
4	Example:								
5	1	Executive Summary	N/A	N/A	–	SL	10th January		
6	2	Question content	Quality systems	1.1	25	FB	9th January	Yes	Discussed minor amendments
7	3	Question content	Health and safety	2.1	5	JS	9th January		
8	4	Question content	Human resources	3.1	5	EJ	9th January	Yes	Signed off by HR director
9	Etc								
10									
11	25	Pricing proposal	Costs	12.1	50	MM	10th January		Draft version seen on 8th Jan
12	Etc								
13									
14									
15									
16									
17									
18									
19									
20									
21									
22									

Sheet1 Sheet2 Sheet3

Coach contributors on the items they own

It's also a great idea, if the tender document shows question or section 'weight-ings', to include them in the outputs matrix. A weighting is the percentage score given to a question/response by the buyer. By showing the weightings in the outputs matrix, contributors can easily see the relative importance of their content to the overall bid.

Other pieces of advice or guidance can also be included in the outputs matrix to aid contributors. For instance, I often include a column showing target word count or number of pages. And, if there are any important sales messages to get across in the response, I include them here too (for example flexibility, innovation, reliability, etc).

As with the timetable, circulate the outputs matrix as early as possible in the process. Try to spend some time with each individual contributor, mak-ing sure they all fully understand your expectations for their submissions, and checking that they feel confident in completing each task.

As the process unfolds and you start to receive content, take the time to review individual contributions as they arrive, to be sure they are of the right standard.

Update the outputs matrix, noting any new deadlines you allocate to work that needs to be revised or reworked. (This might have an impact on your overall timetable – keep the two documents coordinated.) Once you are happy that work is complete, mark it as such on the matrix (I often use colour-coded text for this) and prepare to add it to the response template, as described later.

Step 4 – prepare a content checklist (not always necessary)

A content checklist helps you to ensure that all of the customer's detailed requirements are acknowledged somewhere in your response document. It's a 'map', cross-referencing requirements to responses. Whether or not you need one is really down to how the customer's tender document has been constructed.

It might be easier to explain this through an example. The customer's document might state: *Suppliers must provide a 24-hour service. In the case of a minor incident, 95% of technicians must be available within 1 hour. In the case of a major incident, 50% of technicians must be available within 48 hours.* But in the list of questions to answer it might simply say: *Provide information on your business continuity procedures.*

Your response to this question must acknowledge the specific requirements that the buyer has included (ie the need for a 24-hour service, and variable levels of recovery after an incident, etc), not just the general subject matter covered by the question.

To be sure this happens, your checklist shows the contributors where to look for the requirement detail. They can then be sure to include information on how this requirement would be met when constructing their response. So, in the above example, your content checklist would include the extract shown in Table 5.1.

TABLE 5.1 Extract from a sample content checklist

Question number	Detailed requirement
17. Provide information on your business continuity procedures	Page 6 of ITT, section 13.2 *Suppliers must provide a 24-hour service. In the case of a minor incident, 95% of technicians must be available within 1 hour. In the case of a major incident, 50% of technicians must be available within 48 hours.*

Of course, there will be times when several requirements need to be acknowledged under a single question. They simply need to be added into your content checklist under the relevant question. Contributors will then need to ensure that they acknowledge all requirements and state how they will each be met, in their response.

When you'll need a content checklist

If the customer states a requirement and asks for your response immediately after it, you will not need a content checklist. If, however, the requirements and questions are given separately, you will need to create a checklist to be sure you have not missed any important requirement.

Depending on the complexity of the opportunity, it is possible to combine the outputs matrix and content checklist into one document, so that contributors have all their instructions together in one place. Just make sure it doesn't get too complicated or unwieldy!

Formatting and populating the document

Step 5 – prepare a response template (must-do)

You're now ready to start preparing the document that will contain all your content – the bid response document itself. Clearly, this is a very important document, and you'll need to think carefully about how to construct it.

Sometimes buyers are very clear about how they wish you to construct the response and you will have strict instructions about what to do. They might even provide a template. If this happens, great. Just be sure to follow their instructions to the letter.

In other cases you might have no guidance from the buyer at all and you'll have to start completely from scratch. Of course, as with all things, the reality is likely to be somewhere in between these two extremes.

What you normally find is that the tender document is laid out as follows:

- an overview of the customer and the opportunity;
- specific requirements;
- instructions for suppliers;
- supplier capability questions;
- proposed or sample terms and conditions.

A good response document needs to include (at the very least):

- cover page;
- contents table;
- executive summary;
- your response to requirements;
- your pricing proposal;
- references;
- appendices.

Bearing these in mind, here's a list of guidelines to help you to create your document template:

1 Don't use the customer's entire tender document and just add your responses to it (unless the customer specifically instructs it, of course). The last thing buyers want to do is to wade through their own text before finally arriving at your response content. Instead, using your own logic, create a document outline that includes everything in your outputs matrix.

Your cover page needs to include:

- the customer's name (this should appear first, or more prominently than your company name);
- your company name; name and/or number of the tender; date of submission;
- contact details (these can go in the contents page or executive summary page if you prefer);
- a disclaimer (see the box below).

A word of advice here about customer logos: make sure you're not going to infringe any trademark or copyright laws by putting the customer's logo on the cover of your bid. A quick question to your buyer asking permission to reproduce the logo is all it needs.

Disclaimer text

'This proposal is completed in good faith. Information contained herein is strictly confidential and should not be used or divulged other than in connection with this PQQ/proposal/ITT/RFP [delete as appropriate]. It is supplied on the understanding that it shall not be supplied to a third party without the prior written consent of [your company name here].'

---

2 Next should be a contents table. This should never take up more than one page. If it does, you're including too much detail on it. In most cases, level one headings are fine here.

3 Always start the body of the document with an executive summary, even if you're not asked for one. (See Chapter 6 for more on this.)

4 When creating the main response to requirements content, avoid the temptation to keep in the customer's list of requirements and to simply write 'acknowledged and understood' underneath each one, or something similar. This will not impress the buyer, and will not show how you will meet the requirements. This is where your content checklist comes in, if you're using one. Requirements need to be addressed specifically somewhere in the document. Think of the best way to represent this: perhaps in the questions, or in a specific section 'How we will meet your requirements'.

If the customer's document has section numbering, retain it so that evaluators can see how your responses map back to the original tender document. Of course, this sometimes means starting your response at a section number other than one! This is fine; simply include a sentence on your contents page that explains that you are matching the original numbering in the tender document.

5 If the customer's document has no numbering system, consider creating one of your own. This is especially useful if you need to cross-refer within your responses; without numbers this is virtually impossible.

It's vital that you 'frame' each page of your document with a header and footer. This has several purposes:

- To remind the reader whose bid they're reading (I always put the bidder's logo at the very least in the top or bottom corner of each page for this purpose!). See 'Step 6 – decide how you're going to present your bid' below for more tips on headers.

- To provide a point of reference in the document (always include page numbers, and include a section name if this is a multi-section document).

- To give the reader useful reference information about this document. If you are not given specific instructions about what needs to be included, I would recommend: the name and reference number (if applicable) of the tender and the words 'In Confidence' (if this is a private sector bid: you wouldn't want this information to end up in the wrong hands), and the date of submission.

6 Often the buyer will give you one or more forms to sign or acknowledge, and to include somewhere in the document (these might be confirmation of non-collusion with other bidders or certification of a bona fide bid, etc). Work these in to a logical place in the document, often at the front (but after the executive summary, of course) or at the back.

7 Include extra information at the end in an appendices section if you need to. However, avoid just tipping a load of generic marketing material in at the end, 'just in case'. Buyers often don't read appendices anyway, so if something's important find space for it in the main body of the document.

8   Finally, if you have time, transfer the owners and deadlines from your outputs matrix into your master document so that you can see at a glance who has yet to make their contribution and whether or not they are out of time.

Getting Microsoft Word to work for you

Word is a great tool for constructing documents like a bid response – when you use it properly! If you don't, it can really hinder progress, or add significant time and frustration into the bidding process. My advice is to make sure that whoever is going to own the master document becomes a Word expert pretty quickly! Send the person on a course or buy him or her a book, but at the very least the Word expert will need to be able to master:

- the track changes function;
- auto-numbering;
- style templates;
- tables;
- page and section breaks;
- headers and footers;
- table of contents (only possible if you use the style template correctly!).

Step 6 – decide how you're going to present your bid (must-do)

Before you cut and paste a single word into your response template, think about document presentation. Unless your bid is submitted via an e-portal as text only, this is a really important part of the process, because your document needs not only to stand out from the other bids, but also to be reader-friendly. This is equally important if your bid is to be submitted in hard or soft copy.

Here are a few tips on how to make the style of your document as good as its substance, and to help you to get on the good side of the reader.

Use a reader-friendly font

Occasionally your instructions will specify a font type, font size and line spacing protocol to follow. Make sure you do as requested; there's bound to be a reason for this instruction. I once had to write a bid in 14-point Arial because the main evaluator had a visual impairment and this was the smallest font size he could comfortably read.

If there are no instructions given, go for a minimum of 11-point size, and use a sans-serif font such as Arial.

White space

It's all right to have lots of white space in your document; it helps readers to focus on the words in front of them. Left-justify your text, to create a ragged right-hand edge – reading experts say that it helps readers to progress to the next line without losing their place. If you think it helps, use 1.5 line spacing in your document, too.

Single-sided versus double-sided printing

I'd go for double-sided, every time, unless you have strict instructions to the contrary. Think of the environment!

Housing your bid

Unless it's an electronic submission via a website, e-mail or CD/memory stick, you'll need to think about how you are going to produce and submit your bid. Will you choose a ring binder, or will you bind it? Maybe you'll insert the pages into a presentation folder? Will there be dividers in your document? If so, will they be plain, or will you use them to introduce some pictorial interest, or to reinforce sales messages? Whatever you decide, you'll need to prepare your documents with your final presentation method in mind.

If you are submitting via CD or memory stick, this still gives you a good opportunity to present your bid in an interesting and eye-catching way. Perhaps you could produce a CD sticker and insert, or house your memory stick in a branded box?

Check whether your instructions include any specific instructions about how the bid should be housed and plan accordingly.

My advice is to go for the highest specification presentation materials that you can afford (appropriate to the size of the opportunity, of course), to show the buyer that you have invested in this bid and have an appetite to win it.

Example – making your bid stand out from the crowd

I once housed a bid in a tailor-made box that had been created using the customer's colour scheme and branding. We were the incumbent, but competition was fierce for this lucrative contract. We needed to show how important this contract was and just how much we wanted to retain it.

Into the box we added extras like a magazine, created to show the results of focus group research, and a DVD produced by the account team to show the work that had already been done, and the future innovations that were planned. We also put in copies of compliments that we had received from end-users of the service, to show how much our service was valued. The bid folder was designed using the customer's branding, and each section of the bid was fronted by a divider that showed a photograph of a member of staff already engaged in delivering the service, with a quote from that person to show his or her past successes or aspirations for the future.

We know, from feedback given at the end of the bid, that ours was the first opened, simply because of the intriguing nature of the box it was housed in and the interesting way in which we presented our material. I believe that we then set the standard for other bidders. (We won this one, by the way.) Clearly, a lot was invested in the presentation of this bid – but then again we had a lot to lose.

If you feel it's appropriate to try something different or quirky that will get you noticed, by all means go for it, especially if you operate in a less traditional sector where innovation and creativity are prized attributes. But don't overstep the mark and tip too far into gimmicky; your buyer might not like it! Judge carefully, checking with the buyer if necessary. This is particularly important if you plan to adapt or use the customer's brand or logo in the presentation of your bid. You don't want to be accused of a trademark infringement (it has been known!). A quick call to the buyer could help you to avoid embarrassment or worse, later on.

Cover story

Your cover will say an awful lot about you, so make sure it's only saying good things. Once again, put yourself in the buyer's shoes. Which bid would you reach for first, when they're all spread out in front of you on the table? Obviously, there are no guarantees, but I'm pretty confident that a thoughtfully presented document with an interesting cover would grab your attention ahead of a scruffy black and white tome sporting the customer's (slightly amended) original ITT front cover.

Make your cover look as appealing as possible, using colour and pictures to create interest. If you can work your bid theme (see Chapter 6) into a 'strapline' for your bid, why not include this on your front cover too?

Dividers

Where the bid response is longer than about 20–25 pages in total, I would consider breaking it up into sections, for ease of navigation by the reader.

Use section breaks in your document to ensure that new sections always begin on an odd-numbered page, so that when you print it out it can easily be divided up. This might leave you with some blank pages. Either mark them as intentionally blank, or space out your document accordingly.

Dividers are a good device through which to further promote your key sales messages, so don't just leave them blank. You could include your bid theme, some of the high-level benefits, photographs of your company in action, customer testimonies, staff biographies... there are loads of possibilities. Keep reminding the buyer whose bid it is they're reading, and why you should be selected over other bidders.

Match the dividers with your cover to create a uniform look for your bid.

Tailored bid header

In a similar vein, customize your bid response with a colour header that includes your logo and the bid theme strapline if you have one. It really does make a big difference to the look and feel of the final document. Again, match it to other bid presentation elements for a consistent look.

Step 7 – populate your response template (must-do)

Once you've decided on the format, set up your style template accordingly. Be meticulous and stick to these styles when you cut and paste content into your document, to avoid the mishmash of font types and sizes that will inevitably occur if you don't.

Assuming you're now ready to start putting your content in, here are my document construction guidelines:

1 Don't underestimate just how long and potentially frustrating the construction of the document can be. Make sure you leave sufficient time to complete this task.

2 Don't 'bank' content too early. It's tempting to start putting in content as soon as it arrives, regardless of its quality. Only when you've been through a review/amend/sign-off cycle with the

contributor of a piece of writing should you commit it to your document. Of course, this cycle may need to be repeated several times before you can finally 'bank' it. Don't despair – this is the lot of the bid manager!

3 Save regularly! There's nothing worse than the moment when your computer crashes and you realize you haven't hit the 'save' icon for an hour or two. I'm sure you'll know this feeling; you really want to avoid it when you're preparing a bid. Instigate a manual routine or set up your auto-save function so that you never lose more than 15 minutes' work. Also, keep a back-up on your network, a disk or a memory stick at the end of every day so that, if your machine fails to boot up the following morning, all is not lost.

4 Think about version control. Keep a 'master' version of the response document, and have one person take responsibility for its management. Ask contributors to send stand-alone pieces that are individually referenced so that they can quickly and easily be dropped into the master document. (Avoid sending them the response template and asking them to drop their piece into the right place – this is inefficient for both you and them.) At the end of each day, save your master document as the next version number, so that, if your document gets corrupted or a bug is introduced, you have older (uncorrupted) versions you can go back to.

5 Break up the document into manageable chunks. Whether you actually need to do this will depend on the size and complexity of your response document. If there are clear section headings, then add section breaks to ensure each one starts on a new page. You might also consider creating separate files for each section, especially if you're including lots of photographs or images and your master document starts getting big, or slow to save.

6 Collect and label appendix information as you go. You'll find that contributors love to send you 'extras' and then ask for them to be 'put in at the end', as appendices. This is fine, but remember my earlier advice that readers often don't look at appendices. Be sure there isn't a way to include the content in the main document. If you are going to include them, I suggest that you start a table of appendices and collect up the corresponding content in a separate folder. Ensure each piece of information is clearly titled and labelled (appendices often contain baffling tables of unidentified data!), and shows the relevant appendix number, along with your company

name, at the very least. If you are required to submit electronically, a neat way of presenting your appendices is to embed appendix documents into the appendix table (see Figure 5.3). Consult 'Help' within Word if you're not sure how to do this – I promise it'll be worth the few minutes it takes to work it out.

FIGURE 5.3   An example of appendix documents embedded into a table

Appendix number	Appendix name
1	Health and safety policy Health & Safety policy.doc
2	Quality accreditation certificate Quality certificate.doc
3	Project plan Project plan.xls

Submitting on time

Step 8 – prepare for the deadline (must-do)

Bid deadlines are notoriously short – any experienced bid manager will tell you that there's never enough time to do everything as well or in as much detail as you'd like.

So how should you view deadlines, and what do they really indicate?

Buyers often deliberately set short deadlines; maybe it's part of the test, or maybe they're under huge pressure themselves to find a solution fast. (Be particularly aware of the classic 'New Year deadline' scenario. Many a buyer sends out a tender during Christmas week, with a deadline in the first week of January. Merry Christmas, buyer!)

Whatever the reason, there's no use in wasting energy getting angry or annoyed about a short deadline; the buyer sets the timeframe, and you simply have to stick to it.

So, if the time available seems impossibly short, you'll need to think long and hard about whether or not you should bid. Maybe the process is 'wired' towards an incumbent or preferred supplier? Maybe you were only sent the tender documents late into the process because the buyer needed another supplier to make up the numbers? Maybe you left it too late to get going on the process?

Delivering your bid on deadline day

Your timetable must accommodate the process of getting your document to the customer on time. Right at the beginning of your planning, decide how you will deliver your submission, and then make the necessary arrangements.

If you need to submit a hard copy, will you deliver it yourself, use a courier or send it by post? Allow more than enough time and try to eliminate any risk. Have a plan B if at all possible.

If you need to submit electronically, this will normally mean one of three things:

1 You are required to e-mail your submission. If this is the case, make sure you know what size limitations exist on outgoing e-mails at your end and on incoming e-mails at the customer's end. If you think that your files will be too big, investigate using zipping software, or converting your files to pdfs before sending them on. Consider password-protecting the files, just in case they fall into the wrong hands accidentally.

2 You are required to send an electronic copy by disk or memory stick. It sounds obvious, but make sure you've got disks and/or memory sticks, as appropriate, and make sure your software works! Use password protection for files submitted this way too.

3 You are required to use an e-procurement site. Increasingly, tenders are issued via this route. In theory, these are paperless processes, with buyers posting their requirements via a secure website, which suppliers are invited to access via secure registration procedures. Suppliers submit their response via the website, either by typing their response directly into the website or by uploading documents there. Because these can be fiddly to use, bid managers often work offline

(that is, away from the e-procurement site) and then cut and paste, or upload the documents, near the end. This is a good idea, but I recommend taking time early in the process to understand completely the way that the site works. Tutorials, webinars or conference calls are often offered to bidders at the beginning of an e-procurement process to show them how the site works. Take the support offered unless you're 100 per cent confident you know what you're doing.

During the process, a countdown clock often sits in the top corner of the screen – always a painful reminder of how little time is left. Beware the nightmare of these sites on deadline day – often, as every supplier is trying to upload their documents in the final hour before the deadline, the site runs incredibly slowly or keeps crashing. Be organized, and plan to get ahead of the 'rush hour' traffic (one hour before the deadline). Remember, the website will be taken offline or the option to submit withdrawn the second the deadline is passed, so if you fail to complete on time you will not be included in the evaluation process and you run the risk of all your efforts being wasted.

Asking for more time

Regardless of the story behind an impossible deadline, remember this piece of advice: never ask for a deadline extension. Buyers will always view this as a reflection of your general capability. If you can't get a bid in on time, will you be any more reliable in delivering the product or service you're bidding for? So even the process of asking for more time (even if you do go on to meet the deadline) can deliver a fatal blow to your submission.

Submitting early

In the public sector, there is no advantage to your submission arriving early. This is because the buyer is not allowed to open the documents until the specified deadline time has arrived. So, if the deadline is 5 pm on a Friday, they cannot open any of the parcels or view e-mailed documents until after that time on that date. And, because you are usually asked to submit hard-copy documents in an unmarked parcel that cannot identify your company, no one would ever know that you had sent it in early anyway. No points to be gained, I'm afraid.

In the private sector, however, things are very different. Buyers are not bound by the same rules and can open submissions when they like! They are often tempted to have a peek at documents as they arrive, so there can be a definite advantage in submitting early, since yours might be the first bid the buyer looks at.

Just a word of caution about submitting too early, though. Bids are dynamic processes, and occasionally the buyer will add in a new requirement, provide the answer to a pivotal question or alter some key piece of information towards the end of the process. If you've submitted early, it might not be possible to amend, retract or add to your submission. Even if your bid is complete, and there's truly nothing more you could do to improve it (and I've never known anyone be in this position!), hang on to it, and don't submit more than 48 hours in advance of the deadline – just in case.

Beware the 'unmarked package' instruction

The majority of public sector bids will require you to submit your bid in an unmarked envelope or package and will often provide a label for you to use.

It sounds simple, but it's easy to trip up on this. For instance, if you use a courier, make sure that they don't affix a docket bearing your name and address to your plain parcel. And, if you normally send your package through your post room team, who use a franking machine – with your company's name on it – maybe it's worth a trip to the post office this time, but make sure they don't affix a label bearing the sender's address. Why not deliver it in person, to be absolutely sure?

Apparently, this instruction is given to prevent buyers from knowing who has submitted bids until the moment all the packages are opened – at the same time, and only after the deadline has passed. You must go to great lengths to make sure you adhere to this instruction. I know of too many instances where a bidder has been disqualified for not meeting this request. Don't let it happen to you.

Late submissions

In the public sector a late submission will almost certainly mean disqualification, I'm afraid.

If you have a good relationship with the buyer, and you're stuck in traffic 10 minutes away from the submission address, with 5 minutes left until the deadline, a call to explain your predicament might just work (or it might not – this is at the buyer's discretion). Normally, the evaluation panel meets immediately after the deadline passes; if your parcel is not there, you're out.

In the private sector, there may be a little more leniency, but I wouldn't bet on it. Buyers hate it when their instructions are ignored. You'll have put a severe dent in your credibility if you submit late, unless you've got a very good excuse.

Step 9 – final pre-production review (must-do)

Of course, before you can complete this step, you need to be confident that your content is as good as it can be and that your document is not merely a compliant one but a winning one. This process of content creation and review is covered in Chapter 6.

You may therefore wish to read ahead before coming back to these final steps, which will help you through the last anxious hours and minutes (maybe seconds) before the deadline arrives and you need actually (or virtually) to hand over your submission.

What's missing?

This is where your outputs matrix comes into its own (again). It's now your checklist to help you make sure that everything is included in the final submission. So tick everything off the outputs matrix as you prepare to print, or save to file, or upload to the procurement website.

Proofread

This stage so often gets missed out, but it can save some real embarrassment later. I've seen howlers left in final bid submissions: things like 'Will have to make something up for this', or 'No idea what should go here', or the classic mistake of leaving another customer's name in a cut-and-pasted section (always an evaluator's favourite – see below). And of course there are tales told in bid management circles of bored or mischievous contributors putting in rogue swear words or messages of support for their football team, etc, etc! I think you'd quite like to remove them, wouldn't you?

At the very least, run it through spell-check – hardly infallible but better than nothing. Why not get someone who's not been involved in the bid at all to cast an eye over it?

Customer name check

Customers can be fussy about little things like their name being spelt correctly, so I'd advise a special check on this. If there's any doubt about how to refer to a customer, look back at their original documents and replicate their language. Only abbreviate or use a diminutive or shortened version of their name if they do so themselves.

Also make sure that no one has inadvertently left in another customer's name (this happens a lot when old bids or proposals are used as a starting point). Even worse, 'Customer's name here' comments suggest that you churn out the same document time after time.

Pagination

A visual check this one, to make sure that headings are still sitting on the same page as their paragraphs and that you don't have pages with one stranded heading or sentence on them. Also check that tables and graphics haven't covered up headers and footers anywhere in the document.

Table of contents

Only when your pagination check is complete should you run your final pre-production task – the table of contents update.

If you've used the Word style template, this is a simple job (though beware stray body text somehow promoting itself to a heading!).

Otherwise, you'll have to create a table, add in the headings manually, and check and drop in the page numbers. Honestly, that's just a waste of your time. It's well worth getting to grips with Word properly to avoid the stress of having to create a last-minute contents table.

Step 10 – production and delivery (must-do)

This step can be the most stressful part of the process, I'm afraid.

Your printer will almost certainly run out of toner mid-document, or your computer will freeze up or crash. The internet will stop working or your e-mail account will be inaccessible.

You'll have to find your own way of coping with these challenges, but the end is in sight. Of course, if you've managed your timetable well, you'll hopefully have plenty of contingency time before the deadline.

Because every bid is slightly different, there's no definitive checklist that I can give you here. But these are the main things to think about:

1 Check that you have included everything in your submission. Is every page printed and every file uploaded? Does the CD or memory stick that you made work in another computer?

2 Double-check that you have followed the instructions to the letter. Have you got the correct address, or used the address label provided? Have file naming conventions been observed? Have you included the right number of hard and soft copies? Have you included all required files and actually pressed 'submit' on an e-bid?

   And immediately the bid leaves your hands...

3 Seek reassurance that your bid has been received by the customer. If the bid is going in hard copy and you're not handing it over in person, I recommend that you ring or e-mail the buyer to tell them that your parcel is on its way, and to give an expected arrival time. Check with your courier to ensure that the parcel was signed for in time. It's also worth a double-check once the deadline has passed, to make sure that it has actually arrived and is safely in the buyer's hands. If the bid is going via e-mail, it's a good idea to request acknowledgement or even to use your mail system's 'confirm receipt' option. In the case of an e-bid, you should get an automatic receipt from the system; I always take a screen shot of this, for safe-keeping.

Step 11 – reflect, and then celebrate (must-do!)

Maybe it's just me, but the sense of relief that I expect to feel straight after I submit a bid never seems to arrive.

There's always a niggling feeling that you might have forgotten something, or that perhaps you could have worded something in a more positive light. In a way this is a good thing; when you write bids and proposals, you should aim for perfection. But be kind to yourself, too. You've just completed a big and important task that could win your business a new contract.

Make a quick list of things that you'd do differently next time: things that might make the process run more efficiently or quickly; things that will give your next bid more credibility; ideas that will improve the presentation of your next submission...

In Chapter 10 we'll look at how this insight, married with the feedback from the buyer, will give you a new starting point for your next bid.

But, for now, do something to celebrate your achievement. Thank those who have helped you and make sure you keep them informed of the final outcome. And don't forget to pat yourself – as bid manager – on the back.

SUMMARY

Using a disciplined approach to managing your bid will pay huge dividends. Not only will your bid be fully compliant and ready on time, but you should also be able to avoid too much burning of the midnight oil.

Every bid needs a leader, someone who's in charge of getting everything done at the right time to the highest possible standard. Appoint one, and make sure everyone involved knows who this is.

Start by creating a timetable to help you to manage your bid; otherwise you'll run out of time, patience or energy, or all three. Plan your approach carefully and create your response template and other tools before you start writing anything.

Keep the customer's instructions to hand at all times, and follow them to the letter.

When it's all over, take time to reflect on what you've just achieved, and remember to thank all those involved. Make a list of the things that you'd do differently next time – and do them differently next time.

What to write and how to write it

06

THIS CHAPTER COVERS:

- The kick-off meeting – turning ideas into an action plan

- Preparing a winning executive summary

- Creating the content for your bid

We have now reached the part in the process where you need to decide exactly what you're offering the customer and how it will meet the customer's needs (your 'solution'). Following on from that point, you need to decide how you're going to present that solution in writing.

It can be extremely daunting to be faced with a blank page and a blinking cursor, and the knowledge that you have only a limited amount of time to try to commit your ideas to paper. But please avoid the temptation to 'just get something down in writing', just so that you feel you've started your bid. If you prepare well, your document will be so much easier to write. I can promise that. So turn off your computer again; it's still not quite time to commit pen to paper (virtually, or otherwise).

In the last chapter we talked about including a kick-off meeting in your timetable. It's now time to call that meeting and draw up your solution. Then you can start writing.

The kick-off meeting – turning ideas into an action plan

The kick-off meeting is one of the most important events within your timetable, and will dictate and influence everything that follows. This is the meeting in which you'll set your 'winning strategy', a plan to meet and exceed all the customer's requirements and to determine just why your solution should be selected over all the other submissions.

For this session to work effectively, you'll need the full attention of all the people who might contribute to the design and delivery of your solution. Schedule the meeting at a time when everyone can attend in person; make sure attendees realize how important it is to be there (in body and spirit) and hold it in a place that encourages creativity and fresh thinking. Ask attendees to turn off their mobiles or – radical – make them leave them outside the meeting!

Provide lots of Post-it notes and flipchart paper to capture ideas on, and biscuits and drinks to keep your contributors motivated throughout. How long it takes will depend on the complexity of the requirements and your solution, but make sure you schedule more than enough time. You need to complete all the tasks shown below in this meeting; make sure your contributors can stay until they're all done.

For this meeting you will need:

- the customer's original tender documents;
- your SWOT diagram (showing your strengths, opportunities, weaknesses, threats);
- your outputs matrix;
- your content checklist, if you're using one;
- your bid timetable;
- all potential contributors to the bid;
- Post-it notes and flipchart;
- biscuits and drinks!
- plenty of time.

Here is a list of your kick-off meeting tasks. Tackle them in this order.

Task one – introduce the customer's vision

The customer's vision is their long-term, high-level, aspirational objective for themselves. It's often (but not always) included in their original document, but should always be easy to find via their website or other literature as a one- or two-sentence statement or strapline. You need to find this vision statement as part of your preparation for this meeting.

Before the kick-off meeting starts, stick the customer's vision statement on the wall in your meeting room, so that all your attendees see it from the moment they enter the meeting. Introduce it right at the beginning of the session, and keep referring back to it. Your solution should support and enhance the customer's vision in a demonstrable way.

Recognizing the customer's vision and working it into your bid submission are the first step in demonstrating that you are customer-focused. So start the meeting by spending just a couple of minutes talking about the importance of the customer's vision, and keep coming back to it as the meeting progresses, to make sure everything that is being proposed is in line with it.

Task two – identify the customer's key challenges and requirements for this bid

The buyer will have very specific reasons for putting this contract out to tender, and again you'll need to have identified these in advance of the meeting.

Reasons will vary hugely from opportunity to opportunity and from sector to sector. To give you some ideas of what to look for, they might include:

- cost reduction;
- improvement in quality;
- improvement in end-user satisfaction;
- regulatory or legislation changes;
- capacity increase (higher volumes or increased opening hours, perhaps);
- innovation;
- reduction of customer 'churn' (customers moving away);
- increase in diversity of offering (adding new products or services);
- replacement of the previous or incumbent supplier.

Normally, there are two or three key challenges that the buyer wants to address, and they're pretty easy to spot in the customer's document. Note these down, ready for the kick-off meeting.

Once you've identified the obvious ones, have another look, this time reading between the lines. Go online to research recent news stories about this customer or their sector; what challenges are they and their competitors facing? Better still, if you know the buyer or if you are invited to a supplier briefing (a meeting where the buyer goes over the tender process face to face with suppliers), try to delve a little deeper into the buyer's long-term objectives and find out what other, less obvious problems they would like to solve when selecting a supplier. Often, the winning bid is the one that addresses these smaller concerns as well as the major challenges.

You'll normally find between two and four key challenges that you'll need to discuss in the kick-off meeting. These challenges are also vital to the solution you are about to design and should dictate the way that you design it. Write each one on to its own piece of flipchart paper.

After you've discussed the customer's vision in your kick-off meeting, move straight on to a discussion about the key challenges. Introduce them all; then begin to deal with them one by one. At this stage, I normally ask the bid team to start thinking about how they can solve the challenges, and get them to put ideas on Post-it notes that can be stuck up next to the relevant challenge. In this way, experts from different parts of the business feed in their own expertise in relation to each challenge.

This is the point at which the team starts to design the practical solution for the bid. They'll be starting to think about the people, processes and systems that will be needed to meet the customer's requirements, but all this will now be done in the context of having identified the customer's challenges.

Make sure that one function's solution does not create extra cost or operational difficulty for another function. (For example, if your operational team need to bring in specialist skills, could the HR function find and recruit them in the required timescales? Or, if you need to purchase and house specialist equipment, is there space in your current premises, and who would maintain it?) Debate these issues and keep a note of any additional costs, repercussions or drawbacks that they might introduce into your model.

At this point, revisit the SWOT diagram that you prepared when you were deciding whether or not to bid. This will remind you of all the factors that originally influenced that decision. Most will be positive, but some will be negative. Make sure you discuss and incorporate every single element into your solution. It's just as important to address perceived weaknesses as it is to promote your strengths.

Where you've identified opportunities to add extra value, demonstrate them in a quantifiable way in your solution. Conversely, where you perceive there to be a particular threat (in the form of a competitor's strength, say), you'll need to think of a way to neutralize it or play it down.

Addressing weaknesses and threats

It's tempting to shy away from mentioning your weaknesses in your bid submission, and so much easier to focus on the positive. But buyers are realists, and will be on the lookout for drawbacks, or any part of your solution that might introduce risk. They will also be able to see where your competitors' strengths lie relative to yours. In both cases, it will assist in the evaluation of your submission if the buyer can see that you recognize your own shortcomings and are willing and able to address them in the design of your solution. But how to address them?

Perhaps your weakness is a capacity issue, which can be solved, but will take time and introduce additional cost. In this case, you'll need to demonstrate your plan to increase capacity over a specified timeframe, with quantifiable benefits to the customer by the end of the process. You'll need to address the cost issue; perhaps you would be willing to invest some of the cost or spread it over the contract lifetime.

If your weakness is service-related and your performance metrics aren't as strong as they need to be, you will again need to reassure the buyer that you recognize this situation and are taking steps to address it. Show your action plan, quantify the results you expect and give a realistic assessment of how long it will take.

The main thing to realize is that bland reassurances that everything will be all right will not convince the buyer. You need to be assertive and unapologetic, but most importantly you need to be definite about what is being done to address your weaknesses, by whom, and over what time period. You need to show that this approach will bring demonstrable and quantifiable benefits.

By turning your current weaknesses into future strengths, you will show your adaptability and willingness to change and improve. These are attributes that every buyer is happy to see in a future supplier.

Quite quickly, you'll start to create a customer-focused solution. It might be at a relatively high level to start off with, without much detail. This is fine, but, as the meeting progresses and the solution develops, refer to the customer's documents and your content checklist (if you're using one) to make sure that the team considers the specific requirements detailed within them. The outputs matrix should be referred to at this stage too. Make sure that every contributor ensures that the solution you are building covers in detail the subjects they own in the outputs matrix. In this way, after the meeting, they will be able to commence the writing of their submission from a position of knowledge and confidence.

If it's possible, ask contributors to quantify the effect of their proposed solution so that the likely benefit to the customer can be shown (a cost reduction or a faster service, for instance). This might involve making some assumptions about the customer's current situation. Document these and show them in your bid so that the buyer can see how you've arrived at your conclusions and how you justify your claims.

Keep checking that one person's ideas don't have a negative impact anywhere else in the solution, and that you don't add in anything that the customer just doesn't need. The most important thing at this stage is that you focus principally on what the customer wants to buy, not what you've got to sell.

Once this section of the meeting is complete, you'll have identified how you'll meet and exceed each challenge, and you'll have collected in everyone's ideas about meeting specific requirements. You now have all the elements of your 'storyboard', which tells the story of your solution to the customer.

Task three – create your storyboard: start to identify features, benefits, differentiators and, finally, your bid theme

A storyboard is simply an outline of all the various parts of your offering, brought together. It doesn't need to be fancy or complicated; I normally use one piece of flipchart paper and Post-it notes to create mine. (For more complex solutions, you might create storyboards for each function of your business too – but you'll always need one overall storyboard to encapsulate the whole thing.)

Once it's done, it's a great visual representation of all of the things that have been discussed in the kick-off meeting. It shows how all the elements of your solution come together and why they're included. Every member of the team should work to the storyboard when creating their response, so send them a copy straight after the kick-off meeting, or stick it up in the office where it can't be ignored!

Your storyboard should include the following:

1 It needs to show all the practical things that you are going to do or provide to the customer. These are your solution's **features**. Put these as a list on your storyboard.

2 For each feature, you'll need to 'justify' why you're proposing to deliver the solution in this way, and to indicate why this is a good idea. These are the **benefits** of your solution. Show these alongside

the relevant feature on your storyboard, and quantify them wherever possible.

3 If you believe that you can offer a feature/benefit that is unique, that none of your competitors can claim, you have a **differentiator**. Highlight any differentiators on your storyboard.

4 Finally, your storyboard needs to include your **bid's win theme**. This is the central premise of your bid, the big idea that you want the buyer to notice above everything else. Your win theme must therefore show clear and definable benefits for the customer. In the ideal scenario, your bid theme will be linked to your differentiator, giving the buyer a clear reason to choose you above other bidders.

Sometimes your theme will be blindingly obvious; other times you'll have to look hard for it. Or you might have two factors emerging as win theme contenders. This is all right. You can have more than one, but don't dilute the impact of your theme by trying to over-complicate it.

When searching for your theme, brainstorm with your contributors and ask them to propose a single factor each; then debate them until a clear winner emerges.

If you're scratching your head for a theme for your bid, have a look through the following list for inspiration (remember, to complete your win theme you'll need to demonstrate a quantifiable benefit to the customer):

- innovation;
- creativity;
- flexibility;
- agility;
- reliability;
- quality;
- additional capacity;
- low cost;
- speed to implementation;
- low risk;
- security;
- cost guarantee;
- budget control;
- ease of doing business.

Features, benefits, differentiators – spot the difference

I think it might help here to give some examples of features, benefits and differentiators and to help you to work out how to tell the difference. These three types of sales message are each important in their own way, but it's only when you understand how they relate to each other that you can really start to use them to good effect.

A feature is a fact about a product or service, describing what it is or what it does. Examples include:

- a service that is available 24 hours a day, 7 days a week;
- automatic standby mode on a piece of electrical equipment;
- gloss paint;
- a propelling pencil.

A benefit describes the advantage that a feature gives to the user. It answers the question: *so what?* Examples include:

- 24-hour, 7-days-a-week service – allowing you to stay in contact with your customers at all times;
- automatic standby mode – saving electricity when not in use;
- gloss paint – providing a hard-wearing, wipe-clean surface;
- propelling pencil – never needs sharpening.

Just a word of caution about benefits, though. A benefit needs to be perceived as useful by its recipient, so you need to be sure that any advantages that you describe are relevant to the recipient. Offering a service 24 hours a day, 7 days a week might not be a benefit to a company if they operate a 9 am to 5 pm model and have no need to be in touch with their customers out of hours. In this case, promoting round-the-clock availability is not a benefit and, in fact, could be viewed as an expensive and unnecessary feature. Think carefully about how you present your benefits, then.

A differentiator is a unique benefit: one that isn't offered or delivered by anyone else. You might have a clear differentiator already; perhaps you give a performance guarantee that no one else offers, or you might hold exclusive production rights to a product.

However, in most cases you'll need to look for small but tangible differentiators that you can promote in your bid. These might include such things as:

- being located near to the customer (feature) – so that you can provide an immediate and flexible service (benefit);

- having unparalleled experience in delivering similar services (feature) – quicker results, without risk (benefit);

- providing real-time, secure access to management information (feature) – allowing the customer to see results as they happen (benefit).

The classic differentiator is price, of course, but this needn't be the one that you focus on. The cheapest does not always win.

In reality, often your differentiator is the team that will be providing the solution: the real people with real experience of doing this kind of work. Promote the expertise and knowledge of your team; highlight how this will ensure minimization of risk and maximization of success. This is often the best differentiator of all.

Task four – gain agreement from your contributors for the remainder of the process

By the time your storyboard is complete, your solution design should be pretty much complete, barring elements that require verification outside of the meeting. There are likely to be questions that you need to ask of the buyer, so make a note of these as you go through the meeting, and fire them off as soon as you can after the meeting.

Other elements might require clarification from other parts of the business or from your own suppliers. Again, note these down and assign ownership. Make sure each point of clarification has a single owner and a deadline, and ask for findings to be reported back via you as soon as possible.

As clarifications come back to you, from either the buyer or internal bid contributors, circulate any new information out to the whole bid team so that any impacts on your solution can be identified and addressed as appropriate. (Regular five-minute meetings or conference calls are the quickest and most effective way of discussing these extra considerations after your kick-off meeting. They also help to find out what progress is being made in the actual writing process.) Keep your storyboard up to date as and when any part of the solution changes, and make sure everyone is working to the latest version!

Your kick-off meeting tasks are now complete, and the groundwork is set for a really well-structured and customer-focused bid. Circulate all the relevant outputs from the meeting (timetable, outputs matrix, storyboard) and prepare for the next step of the process.

Preparing a winning executive summary

As soon as possible after your kick-off meeting and whilst everything is fresh in your mind, your next task should be to draft the executive summary. This is a really important part of your document – arguably the most important – so it needs your undivided attention.

The executive summary is often the only part of your bid that some senior decision makers will actually read. It should certainly be the first thing that anyone looking at your bid comes across. If this is your first or only chance to represent yourself and your solution, you can see just how vital it is to include all the right messages in it.

Don't, therefore, be tempted to leave writing the executive summary until the end of the bid process, as most people do. Draft it early on, and refine it as you go, but don't put it off. If you don't believe that you can write it until you have tied down all the details of your solution, then you're not planning to write the right kind of summary!

Your summary needs to include all the key sales messages about your solution, presented in a customer-focused way. You should have all this information following your kick-off meeting, so there's no excuse not to get going right away. A good executive summary is not just a short form of your operational solution. It's a summary of all the reasons why you are the right supplier in this instance: messages you are sending to the buyer to position you ahead of the competition right from the start.

Before we look at the right messages, let's consider what the wrong messages are. Almost all of the executive summaries that I've seen begin in a similar way: 'We'd like to thank you for this opportunity...', quickly followed by: 'ABC Ltd has a long and proud tradition of service excellence. Operating since 1935, we have over 1,000 employees in five locations across the UK...'. Now, put yourself in the buyer's shoes for a second. You've got maybe 12 bids to read and evaluate, each over 50 pages long. It's a Monday morning, and you must have your preliminary evaluation report prepared by close of play Friday. Just at this moment, are you interested in reading that someone is grateful to you for inviting them to submit a bid? Probably not. And is it important to you at the beginning of reading the document to discover that ABC Ltd has over 1,000 employees in five locations? Definitely not! This could be a long, painful process of wading through lots of irrelevant information until you find what you're looking for. Uh-oh.

However, if a bid opens with a statement that clearly indicates that your challenges are recognized and will be resolved, you're suddenly going to be much more interested in what comes next. Hooray!

Buyers are only human beings (yes, really), and will be influenced by well-organized, relevant messages. Your executive summary will set the tone in the buyer's mind for what's to come. If you start in a way that engages buyers and clearly creates a strong picture of a relevant solution, they are likely to be more receptive as they continue through the rest of the bid. Conversely, if you start off with irrelevant padding, the buyer will perhaps expect the rest of the bid to continue in the same way and might not be so receptive. You should always try to keep the buyer onside with your writing, but especially so in the executive summary. But how?

The secrets behind a great executive summary

It's much easier than you think to write a compelling executive summary. I use a five-step approach that makes sure that the resulting piece is tailored and compelling for the reader. Not only that, but because it's structured you won't miss anything out by mistake, nor will you be stuck staring at a blank page, wondering where to start.

The five steps are:

1 *Demonstrate your understanding of the customer's vision.* Begin your executive summary by introducing your awareness of the customer's vision to show that you understand their overall strategic direction. Show how your organization is a good cultural fit with theirs if possible, by stating how your solution supports or is congruent with their vision.

2 *Introduce your win theme.* This is a really compelling and customer-focused statement that shows your big ideas for this bid in a few words. A good win theme statement should be short, snappy and assertive and should always illustrate desirable and quantifiable benefits to the buyer in the form of your 'value proposition' (see Chapter 7 for further detail on what this means). To make it even more attractive to the buyer, try to show these benefits as early as possible. Imagine that you're writing a statement that the buyer will quote to his or her decision-making panel as justification for selecting your bid over all of the others. If it works on this level, you know you've got a good win theme statement.

An example of a bid theme statement

'Our solution will give you a speedy, safe and hassle-free implementation. Project X will be delivered two weeks ahead of schedule, allowing you to begin generating revenue much earlier than expected. Using our unique project management systems, our project management team have successfully delivered two similar projects within the last six months, and your project will carry a greatly reduced risk because of this experience.'

The result will be a summary of customer-focused benefits that will create a receptive and positive mindset in the buyer when progressing to read the detail behind your opening statement.

3 *Address each of the key challenges in the context of high-level specific requirements.* Straight after your win theme statement, begin to show your understanding of the challenges the buyer wants to address by letting this contract (the need to reduce cost, improve quality, obtain additional capacity, etc). List them, acknowledging any specific requirements that are associated with each one (using specified materials, introducing a quality control team, scheduling an overnight shift, etc). Against each challenge, use the following structure to summarize the features, benefits and credibility of your approach:

- What outcome are you going to provide against this need? (The quantifiable high-level benefit)
- How are you going to do it? (Features/description of this part of the solution)
- Where have you done it successfully before? (Proof of the credibility of this solution, and your experience and capability in delivering it).

At this point, it might help if you provide a description of your overall operational solution, so that the customer can envisage your proposed approach to fulfilling the contract. This might include information on location, the key team, technology to be used, high-level processes, etc. If this solution can be represented in the form of a picture or diagram, consider placing such a graphic in this part of your executive summary.

4 *State your commercial headline.* Many people are uncomfortable about showing their price 'too early', before they've had a chance to demonstrate fully the quality of their solution. But from discussions I've had with buyers over the years, since price is so important, even if you try to tuck it away at the back of your document, the buyer will simply look for it almost immediately. So you might as well be up front with it, and take the opportunity to put it in the context of all the benefits that you have identified for the customer. This is your value proposition, a very important part of your bid (see Chapter 7 for further detail). I recommend giving a headline pricing statement at this stage of your executive summary, stating as succinctly as possible the cost of your solution. Alongside this, also include any added value elements (additional benefits that don't cost more), and any investment you are making in the solution yourself (training of staff, project management or other set-up costs). If you are also willing to offer preferential payment terms that will help the customer's cash flow, you could introduce this concept here too.

5 *Summarize.* If you want to give a *brief* description of your organization in the executive summary, then this might be a good place for such a statement, but avoid the temptation to make this into a general brag. Make sure you present features with benefits that are relevant to this customer. If you're not sure whether to include something, put yourself back in the buyer's shoes. Read each sentence and ensure that the buyer's response to it will not be: so what? This is your opportunity to cement a positive mindset in the reader, and to really set yourself apart from the other bidders, who might have put forward a compliant, but less customer-focused, bid. Also consider including in your summary an offer to take up references, to further demonstrate cultural fit and to show your passion and appetite for the challenge ahead. If you felt uncomfortable about not including one earlier, you could always include your 'Thank you for the opportunity' statement here.

Finally, always sign off the executive summary with your name and title and the date of submission, to create the concept of personal ownership and leadership of your proposal.

Writing style tips for your executive summary

This part of the document should be very reader-friendly; remember, this might be the only part of your bid that senior decision makers actually see.

Keep it as short as possible, maybe as little as one page if you can fit all your messages comfortably on one page.

Use short sentences and an assertive language style ('We will...', not 'If selected, we would...').

Avoid vague reassurances ('We hope to improve your order processing speed') or unquantified benefits ('Some of your orders will be despatched earlier'). If you're not careful it looks as though you're deliberately trying to avoid committing to anything definite.

Include a relevant testimony from another customer somewhere in your executive summary to build further trust and reassurance in the reader's mind that you are a 'safe pair of hands'.

Use a two-column structure or other presentational device to make this part of your document really stand out. Use pictures or graphics to lift the text and to create interest. In the past I've created executive summaries in lots of different ways: as a fold-out storyboard, as a glossy magazine, as a separate prospectus-type booklet and as a DVD. Remember, you're trying to create a great first impression on your reader. Choose the right style and device for your audience. If you're in the creative industry, this is a great way of showing the quality of your work.

Executive summary checklist:

1 Is the customer mentioned more than your organization? If not, it is probably not customer-focused enough!

2 Have you put the name of the customer before the name of your organization in most instances?

3 Are benefits mentioned before features, wherever possible?

4 Does it clearly state your offering, how it benefits the customer and proof of your claims?

Creating the content for your bid

This is the stage of the process when the majority of the writing will need to take place. You and your contributors are now faced with the task of writing up your respective parts of the solution, as allocated within the outputs matrix, to fill in the blanks in the response template that you created earlier.

In my experience, this is the part of the process that most bid contributors dread. However, it needn't be daunting; the application of logic and a customer-focused mindset will contribute greatly to a successful outcome.

Try the following approach:

1 Read and reread the question/instructions that you've been given. Make sure you're completely clear about what information you need to impart. There's no need to include everything you know about a subject – just what's been requested in this instance. Stick to the brief! This is one of the golden rules of bidding, so ignore it at your peril.

2 Sketch out the outline of your piece before trying to fill in the detail. Use a logical structure to ensure that all salient points are shown in the right order. Ensure key facts, features, benefits, etc are included at the start of your piece. You might even consider including a summary statement at the beginning of your response (demonstrating compliance to the stated requirement) before you go on to provide further detail.

3 When describing a solution (that is, how you propose to do something), stick to the same formula you used in the executive summary, namely:

   – What outcomes do you envisage? State the high-level benefit(s).

   – How are you going to do it? Introduce the features/description of this part of the solution. Use the questions 'Who?', 'What?', 'When?', 'Where?' and 'Why?' to build your answer.

   – Where have you done it successfully before? Prove the credibility of your solution and your capability to deliver it. You might not want or need to include case study information with every answer, but you should consider either including case study notes (one or two lines that highlight your experience) or cross-referencing to a complete case study elsewhere in your document. See more on case studies in Chapter 8.

4 Keep your answers short and assertive. Use active and not passive language wherever possible. So, instead of saying 'Stock levels will be checked every 24 hours' (passive), say 'Our warehousing team will carry out complete stock-level checks every 24 hours' (active). In the active example, the action is attributed to an owner; in the passive it is not. Using an active style makes your solution much more credible and real.

5 Use graphics to illustrate your point wherever possible. Not only does this break up the text, but it can replace a significant number of words. Plan, therefore, what graphics can be employed before you start writing – it might save you a lot of time and effort! Don't try to over-complicate your graphics; show one key idea in each, and aim for simplicity and ease of reading. Always clearly caption your graphics to ensure readers know exactly what they are looking at.

6 Use plain English when creating your text. In reality, this means using short sentences and writing in straightforward language that even the layperson can understand. (Remember, buyers might not be specialists in your field; they won't be impressed if you try to blind them with science!) Try to avoid jargon, unnecessary adjectives (things like 'really unique'), padding, or fancy words (why say 'utilize' when 'use' is just as good?). Stick to the point, and keep the readers in mind at all times. Don't make it difficult for them to find the information they're looking for.

7 Avoid flattery. As tempting as it might be to try to flatter the reader into giving you a better score, this approach can often backfire. Similarly, making exaggerated claims will set alarm bells ringing in the reader's mind. These two things, flattery and boasting, seem to be at the top of buyers' lists of bid 'sins' (along with waffle). Best to avoid them, then.

8 When you think you've finished, first check your writing yourself. The best way to do this is to read it out loud. You'll spot errors much more easily this way. Then ask someone else to have a look. Make sure this person has also got the question, so that he or she can check that you are actually answering it! If there's someone in your company who can proofread your writing as well, ask this person to whizz a red pen over it. So much better that your proofreader sees your mistakes, not the evaluator.

SUMMARY

Now that the time has come to start writing up your bid, it's important that everyone involved has a good understanding of your bid theme and the 'story' behind your solution.

Your kick-off meeting is therefore one of the most important parts of the whole bid process. Plan for it, get a good night's sleep before it (it takes a lot of energy to run one well), and don't let anyone leave until you've completed all the key tasks around solution development.

Agree a win theme, and obtain agreement from all your contributors to weave it into their submissions. Make sure all your bid contributors are focused on the solution that you've all agreed. Share the storyboard and keep it updated as and when things change.

Draft your executive summary as soon as you can after the kick-off meeting; this is an extremely important output – don't be tempted to leave it until the last minute!

Write for your readers. Customer focus means acknowledging their challenges, and showing them how your approach solves their problems, delivering tangible and quantifiable benefits.

How much?
Pricing your proposition

07

THIS CHAPTER COVERS:

- Budget

- Price

- Value

- The pricing balancing act

- Participating in e-auctions

Ah, the $64 million question: how much? Clearly, I can't actually tell you how much you should charge for your product or service, but this chapter will deal with some pretty important things you should know about as you work out your pricing strategy for your bid.

There are three critical elements at play when you create your commercial offer: budget, price and value. My trusty *Oxford English Dictionary* gives me the following definitions:

- **budget (n):** the amount of money needed or available for a purpose;

- **price (n):** the amount of money expected, required or given in payment for something;

- **value (n):** the importance, worth or usefulness of something.

A good buyer will consider all three of these elements when evaluating a bid, having to balance all three before making the final decision to award. Your job is to make as accurate a guess as possible as to where the balance point between all three lies.

All right, I accept that this is pretty tricky, if not impossible, but it doesn't need to be complete guesswork. Let's start by looking at each element in turn, before putting them back together for our balancing trick.

Budget

Budget range

Before the tender document is put out to the marketplace, the buyer will have a budget for the eventual contract award. It is tempting to think of this in absolute terms (that is, as a single figure). In reality, the budget will be a range, with a lower limit and an upper limit. Clearly, the upper limit is the maximum price that the buyer will want to or will be able to pay. The lower limit is the minimum point at which the buyer, by experience, believes it is necessary for the supplier to deliver the contract if it is to be at a sufficient level of quality or competence.

One of the first things the buyer will do when opening bids is to check the overall price versus the budget range. If you are more than about 10 per cent under or over the budget range, it is likely that the buyer will set your bid aside and look at others first. Too low a price and the perception is that you don't understand the brief, can't deliver against it, or have compromised on quality. Too high a price and the buyer will feel that you have over-specified your solution, or would be unlikely to negotiate a reduction that would bring your price back into the acceptable budget range.

Of course, determining the elusive budget range is easier said than done. Sometimes, especially in the public sector, the buyer will indicate the budget available. In these cases, it is the higher limit that you are seeing. This doesn't mean, of course, that you should automatically price your bid on or at that price point. You'll still need to demonstrate good value and should take the time to determine your most competitive price, using it simply as a checkpoint.

Fixed versus variable budget

If you are selling a commodity and are required to quote for a specific number of items of an agreed quality, you will be able to provide a fixed price quote for the whole job. In this way, the buyer can determine your exact price and plot it within the budget range.

Similarly, if you are selling a service and the requirements are specified (perhaps a set number of hours per month), you will also be able to determine a fixed price, which will again give a clear indication to the buyer of where you sit in the budget range.

It could be argued that this is the easiest type of evaluation for the buyer, although there can still be huge variances in quality for the buyer to determine before the contract can be awarded. But what it does mean is that, once awarded, the buyer knows exactly what will be paid during the contract lifetime, with no surprises.

Some service contracts, however, have variable elements, which means that an overall, fixed price for the contract is much harder to arrive at. Perhaps activity volumes are unpredictable or seasonal. Maybe it's a brand new service and demand for the service is unknown. Sometimes in these situations buyers will set scenarios for you to price against. In other cases, they will ask you for your best estimate and you will need to create your own set of assumptions. (We'll cover this in more detail in the 'Price' section below.)

Either way, the outcome will be a variable budget, which will introduce financial risk for one or other party.

Total cost of ownership

When commissioning a capital expenditure contract, buyers will have the long-term budgetary picture in mind. They will not only look to the initial costs of the capital expenditure, but also bear in mind the ongoing costs of the solution throughout its lifetime, from implementation to disposal. These costs might include service, repairs, maintenance, insurance, depreciation and the like. This assessment of the whole-life budget is known as total cost of ownership (TCO). If the buyer is going to use this model, you may well be asked to provide relevant information about likely future costs (as well as initial expenditure costs) to support this.

How buyers manage budgetary (and contract delivery) risks

Buyers will do their best to push financial risk towards the supplier and will often specify contractual terms to manage this. This is especially pertinent in service-based contracts, although it can apply in commodity contracts where demand for the item(s) is unknown and the volume to be ordered is not fixed.

If you are not willing to accept these (or indeed any) of the terms given at the tender stage, you must acknowledge this fact in your bid submission. However, if this situation arises, I would advise you to contact the buyer prior to making your final bid submission, to ascertain the buyer's position on the stated terms. Will there be any room for negotiation at the final stage? Are they willing to be flexible on terms? (If they are, you are likely to have to give something else away as part of your negotiation, in return.)

Buyers will be cagey at this stage and will not want to commit too much either way, but if they are adamant that the winning supplier must accept the given terms without negotiation you must then weigh up the risk to your own financial situation and proceed with great caution. Be prepared to withdraw from the competition if necessary. Remember the 'big' question from Chapter 4: is it profitable? If this now looks doubtful, recheck all the facts of your original decision in the light of this new information.

Four of the key risks that buyers will be looking for, and trying to mitigate against, are shown below:

1 *Financial instability.* Buyers want to be as certain as possible that the supplier will be able to fulfil its obligations for the lifetime of the contract. They will therefore look at the supplier's recent financial history as an indicator of stability and permanence. This is why you're often asked to provide annual account information. If the buyer perceives there to be sufficient indication of risk, you may be asked to provide a guarantee (perhaps from a parent company or other guarantor) or indemnity against the breach of contract that would arise if you were unable to continue trading.

2 *Contract size versus annual turnover.* In a similar vein, buyers want to know how their contract stacks up against all your other workload commitments. To ascertain this, they often ask for information on your existing customers and corresponding contract values. Of course, buyers' attitudes to risk vary greatly according to circumstance, but be prepared to have an excellent case prepared if this contract would account for more than, say, 25 per cent of your existing turnover. (Although it's not related to financial concern, the flip side of this might come when a contract is an extremely small part of your annual turnover. Buyers may perceive that being a small fish in your large pond might not be good in terms of the level of attention they can reasonably expect. You might have to work hard to overcome this objection.)

3 *Managing the risk of uncertain demand.* A buyer might have a contract to award that contains some uncertainty around how many items will actually be needed, or how much or little a service

TABLE 7.1 Financial risks and possible mitigating actions

Risk	Possible mitigation by the buyer	Possible mitigation by the supplier
Forecast levels of activity don't materialize	Buyer requires set-up costs to be covered by the supplier.	Supplier requires set-up costs to be covered by the customer.
	Buyer specifies in the agreement that volumes are not guaranteed.	Minimum revenue level agreed, so that the supplier pays a set amount, regardless of the actual activity level.
Demand greatly exceeds forecast	Service-level penalties for delays in delivery or reduction in quality.	Terms agreed whereby service levels do not apply when activity levels exceed those forecast by a certain percentage.

might be used. What happens if there is less (or indeed more) demand for the product or service than the buyer expects? (See Table 7.1.) Be aware of the financial risk inherent in any agreement you will eventually have to commit to. Try to think about what would happen if there is more or less work than is forecast. If all the risk ends up with you and the worst-case activity scenario actually happens, you need to be certain your business could withstand the potential fallout.

4 *Managing poor performance.* During the bidding process, the buyer will receive unwavering assurance from all bidders that they can and will meet all their performance obligations in the delivery of the contract. However, buyers will want to protect themselves in the event that this is not the reality once the contract is under way. Some contracts will therefore include some kind of service penalty to protect the customer in the event of any significant underperformance. Look at these penalties very closely and determine: 1) the likelihood of the penalty clause being invoked; and 2) the impact on your revenue and profit if it is. Remember, there may be other costs to consider in the case of a service penalty invocation. If you're not meeting service

levels, then on top of the penalties there may be additional costs that you incur in getting your performance back on track (hiring additional people, or retraining existing staff, for instance). As an aside, if you're operating a contract in the public sector, there are the reputational risks to consider too. You might well find your failures and shortcomings discussed in the public domain. There might even be the cost of a defensive PR campaign to fund. Once again, proceed with caution where there are service penalties in the contract. I have recommended withdrawal from several bidding competitions when it became clear that even minor breaches of service levels, sometimes due to circumstances outside the supplier's control, would result in penalties that would result in the contract becoming a loss-making one. Another method that buyers use to manage performance risk is the 'risk and reward' model, a variation of which is the service credit model. Under this arrangement, the supplier receives a reduced fee for providing the service and is awarded a bonus or credit for either meeting or exceeding service levels. This is a favourite of many buyers, but make no mistake: *you* will be carrying the risk as well as potentially enjoying the reward.

Price

And so to the critical question of price. Whilst the majority of buyers to whom I speak are keen to stress that the cheapest solution rarely wins, it certainly is a major factor in pretty much every buying decision I've ever come across!

You'll already have a pricing strategy, a model that you use for other customers, an idea of where you stand in terms of price in your marketplace. Are you a discount, mid-range, high-quality or premium player? How do your closest competitors market themselves?

These factors will have a great bearing on the opportunities you decide to bid for. Unless you are happy to be flexible with your pricing, be sure that you are striking the right balance against the given evaluation criteria in any bid competition. If you're a premium player, then you are unlikely to win too many competitions that are heavily weighted towards price.

So how do you decide how much to charge? You will already have a pricing model and, unless you are required to quote for a brand new product or service that you've never provided before, you should be able to arrive at an overall figure relatively easily. Even if it's the classic back-of-an-envelope calculation, this figure is important in helping you to determine where you might be in the buyer's budget range, how to promote your value proposition (see the 'Value' section below) and also how you stack up against the competition.

There are two approaches to arriving at your price: bottom-up and top-down.

Bottom-up approach

This is the most traditional way of calculating a price or setting a budget. This method takes the component parts or tasks, allocates a price to each (converting time to cost where appropriate) and then adds up all the parts to arrive at a final figure.

Of course, to arrive at an accurate final figure, you need to work out what all the component parts or tasks are, first. This is one of the main disadvantages of the bottom-up approach. If anything is missed out of the pricing model, its cost will still have to be met once delivery is under way, so you might end up compromising the quality of another part of the process or eating into your margin.

Another disadvantage of this approach comes when task owners each build a little 'extra' into their price, for safety or contingency. The aggregate effect of these extras can result in an overall price that makes you uncompetitive.

However, if well managed, the advantage of this approach is its likely accuracy, especially if the tasks have been costed by those who will deliver them in the end. Task owners should have the best idea of how long a task should take and how much it should cost. Make sure that you sketch out the way the work 'flows' from start to finish, identifying the relationships between separate tasks to ensure that nothing is missed.

Top-down approach

This approach works by starting with a budget figure in mind, an idea of what the job 'should' cost. The overall budget is then broken down for component parts or tasks, and a maximum spend is allocated to each.

The advantage of the top-down approach is the certainty that it brings to the headline price, and the spending controls it dictates at individual task levels. (Of course, you'll still need to fully understand the list of parts or tasks in this model.)

The disadvantages come when task owners claim not to be able to deliver their part of the solution without more money. You might well have to 'rob Peter to pay Paul' in this scenario. If you get to this stage, bring the team together to discuss, debate and justify their requests for a bigger slice of the budget. Try to focus the whole team on understanding exactly what resources they can afford; this will hopefully drive cost efficiency and innovation and help to maintain your competitiveness.

Presenting your price

Whatever you do, don't try to hide your price. Buyers will admit that one of their very first actions is to look at the headline price that each bidder has submitted.

Therefore, to make life easy for the bidder, put your commercial headline in the executive summary (unless instructions specifically prohibit this), alongside your value proposition and high-level benefits. Doing this will give buyers a good indication not only of the price they will pay, but also of the overall value to them of your proposal. If you don't make your price easily accessible, buyers will only get annoyed if they have to dig around elsewhere in the document to find it.

If your instructions clearly state that pricing should be presented separately, consider putting a mini (financial) executive summary at the front of your pricing submission, again showing your headline figure alongside your value proposition and benefits.

Price presentation tip 1 – show your assumptions

Where there are any variables that might make it difficult for the buyer to compare prices between bids, show the assumptions that you've used in your calculations. Buyers prefer clarity (it reduces risk), so if you can show the logic in your pricing model it will definitely win you favour with the evaluators.

If necessary, include several scenarios for the buyer to consider, showing the effect on price of any change in the variables in your assumptions. If you're doing this, however, always pick one scenario for your headline figure, and make it clear that this is what you believe to be the most likely scenario.

At the other end of the spectrum, you might have hit upon an innovative or ground-breaking solution that delivers all the required outcomes but at a reduced price. In this case, there's a danger that the buyer will perceive this solution as too risky to implement (unless you can show evidence of where you've carried it out successfully before), or the buyer might think that you haven't understood the requirements and have therefore designed and priced it incorrectly. If this looks likely, consider submitting a compliant bid (showing how you understand the requirement and could do it the traditional way) along with a variant bid for your innovative solution. Alternatively, show your 'crossings-out' to demonstrate the value of your new approach versus the traditional one.

Compliant solution

Ideally, your price will be within the buyer's budget range so that your solution progresses to the next stage of the competition, for more detailed consideration by the buyer. To make this more likely, start by working out the price of a just-compliant solution, that is, the minimum acceptable level of competence or quality that the buyer would accept. Keep this figure in mind at all times and consider showing this as your 'basic' or 'compliant' price.

Premium solution

You might then choose to add in extra cost to produce a higher-quality outcome, but you will need to be able to quantify this in your value proposition, to justify it. If there's a danger that any improved elements you want to include will tip you more than about 10 per cent over the buyer's maximum budget range, think about presenting this extra value in a different way, maybe as a premium solution. Show your workings-out to demonstrate the integrity of your solution over others.

If you wish to promote a premium solution, with extra functionality for a higher price, make sure that you always first provide a compliant bid, and price it accordingly. In this way, you should remain in the buyer's budget range during the initial evaluation.

The buyer can then choose to consider your alternative option (known as a 'variant bid') in the context of all the other (compliant) submissions, including yours. If you do consider this approach, do make sure that the buyer will accept variant bids before you go to the effort of preparing one.

In any case, a premium of more than 10 per cent is probably unjustifiable in either the public or the private sector (but especially the former), even if significant added value can be demonstrated. This is because it is unlikely that the buyer will be able to access the extra budget required to fund your solution. Be careful, therefore, when submitting variant bids, that you're not wasting time that could be better used in preparing your compliant bid.

Price presentation tip 2 – showing your crossings-out

In some cases, there will be more than one way of fulfilling a service contract or of producing a product. If you have considered alternative ways of meeting the customer's requirements, but have disregarded them for good reason, consider 'showing your crossings-out' by presenting them as potential options, but then giving the case against.

This can be a very effective way of pointing out the flaws in competitors' solutions and of highlighting the benefits and differentiators in your own.

Price guarantees

A quick word on price guarantees. If you're tempted to include such a concept within your bid, be very careful. Buyers are inherently sceptical about the notion that any suppliers would truly guarantee that their price will always be the lowest price. Buyers' perception is that there will be small print to navigate, and that anyway suppliers will always look to wriggle out of such an agreement. In addition, buyers perceive that the burden of researching the market and of proving that cheaper prices exist elsewhere will rest with them. Unless you can come up with a simple and buyer-friendly price guarantee, I would try to come up with another differentiator!

Value

And so to the tricky matter of 'value'. A buyer will determine the value of your solution from the perceived relationship between quality and cost. When buyers are looking for 'best value' they want the highest quality (or capability) at the lowest price.

However, in the public sector especially, the equation relies on you meeting buyers' minimum quality requirements; otherwise they won't be able to justify your inclusion on the final shortlist, however good 'value' your solution appears to be. (This is not always true in the private sector, but it's a good idea to bear it in mind.)

At the other end of the value spectrum, buyers might be willing to pay more for a higher capability, but only up to a certain point, because they'll still need to take their budget range into consideration. If you want them to pay a premium, you'll need to demonstrate clearly what will be gained for the extra spend.

Of course, it's easier to demonstrate the value of a tangible benefit, but intangible benefits (by definition, commercially unquantifiable) do still have a value. Buyers will take both into consideration.

An example of a tangible benefit

Your solution might include a system that can be shown to reduce the amount of raw materials needed for one step of a process. A straight reduction in cost can be identified from this efficiency: a tangible benefit.

An example of an intangible benefit

Your solution might include an improved way of working that increases end-user/customer satisfaction. Although this might lead to increased sales or reduced customer attrition, it would be difficult to say that this happened as a direct result of your improvement. This is therefore an intangible benefit.

Value proposition

Every proposal will have a collection of tangible and intangible benefits the buyer can expect from choosing that solution. It's vital that you work hard to quantify both types of benefits, although if you had to make assumptions to arrive at them be clear what they are.

Your value proposition shows buyers the cost of proceeding alongside the quantified outcomes they can expect (ie the tangible and intangible benefits you have identified). It thereby encapsulates the true value of your proposal to buyers, without them having to work it out for themselves. Many proposals simply don't include any kind of value proposition, because bidders struggle to quantify the quantifiable benefits that their proposal will deliver. It's therefore not surprising that buyers favour bids that include a value proposition, since it makes their task much easier.

Your bids should therefore always include a value proposition, which should be introduced in your executive summary and explored in further detail within your pricing proposal.

Your value proposition should include:

- quantified business improvement(s);
- timing of benefits;
- costs and timing of costs;
- the payback period;

- methods for tracking and measuring results (tangible and intangible);
- added value elements (see below).

If applicable, show lost revenues as a cost, avoided costs as a benefit.

Added value

There are ways that your proposition can become more valuable to your customer even when prices are identical to another competitor's bid. If you can show that the buyer will 'get more' by spending the same amount, you are adding value.

Value can be added in a number of ways. You might be willing to share knowledge or skills with the customer for no extra cost (free consultancy). You might be willing to invest in staff training that would produce an intangible benefit (such as staff morale) to the customer. You might have resources or facilities to which you are happy to give the customer free access. Or you might be willing to spread set-up costs over the lifetime of the contract to help the customer's cash flow. Whatever the 'giveaway' that you are prepared to make, make it as customer-focused as possible.

You must quantify the value that you are adding; this will help the buyer to justify the decision to select your proposal against others. Added value elements are therefore a vital part of your value proposition.

Look for ways to offer added value in all your bids; when price is the main evaluation criterion, even small added value elements could swing the decision in your favour.

The pricing balancing act

So we now know that there are three things that need to be balanced when putting together your price: budget, price and value. Different buyers will look at how these factors balance in different ways, according to circumstance.

If there are no given evaluation criteria (sometimes the case in private sector bids), then assume a straight trade-off between quality and price. From what you know about the customer, how far is this likely to swing one way or the other? I advise making an assumption and then basing your final price on it.

Below are the three most common methods that buyers use to arrive at their preferred balance point.

FIGURE 7.1 The comparative value of bids – simple assessment

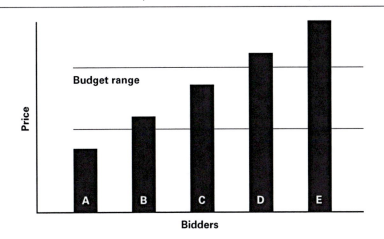

1. Simple assessment

Let's start with the simplest way that buyers might assess the bids received.

Figure 7.1 shows five bids, arranged by price. Budget, as we know, determines the highest acceptable price and the lowest realistic price. Let's assume buyers will disregard any bid that falls more than 10 per cent outside of the range (A and E in Figure 7.1). The remaining bids, all acceptable in terms of price, now need to be compared for value. Bidder D, whilst just above the budget range, might well have the strongest value proposition, and the buyer might choose to negotiate to reduce the price to within budget, whilst retaining the majority of the benefits. However, it is most likely that the award will go to B or C, depending on who has the stronger relative value proposition. Of course, the difference in value must be worth the extra cost in the buyer's opinion.

2. Weighted criteria assessment

In order to assist in the calculation of value, the buyer might well introduce weighted criteria into the assessment. This is very common practice in the public sector, allowing buyers to determine 'best value' or the 'most economically advantageous tender' (MEAT).

In the simplest terms, these criteria could be quality and price, although the same model can accommodate multiple criteria. For example:

Let's say that the weighting for quality was 40% and for price 60%.

Bid X scores 60 marks out of 100 for quality, with a price of £/€/$95,000.

Its weighted calculation is:

$60 \times 40\% = 24$ for quality

$100 \times 60\% = 60$ for quality (as the lowest bidder, it receives full marks for price)

Total score = 84

Bid Y scored 75 marks out of 100 for quality, with a price of £/€/$100,000.

Its weighted calculation is:

$75 \times 40\% = 30$ for quality

$95 \times 60\% = 57$ for price (as a higher-priced bid, its price is scored relative to the lowest. The calculation is £/€/$95,000 ÷ £/€/$100,000 $\times 100 = 95$)

Total score = 87

Bid Y is therefore the winner, despite being more expensive.

The value of the difference in price has been taken into account, and deemed to be sufficient to justify the award being made to the more expensive bidder. The buyer has identified the 'most economically advantageous' or 'best value' tender. This is a clear example of how the cheapest bid does not always win.

3. Multiple weighted criteria assessment with conditions attached

The above example included just two criteria, quality and price, but often buyers will introduce other criteria that are important to them, such as information security, date of delivery, environmental performance, etc.

Whatever the list of criteria, you should always be aware of the relative importance given to each, but also whether or not there are any qualifying conditions to be met as well. Sometimes, buyers will introduce pass marks into performance criteria, to be sure that minimum standards are met by all bidders. This also eliminates bidders who are cheapest only because they have skimped on meeting the required standards.

TABLE 7.2   Example of weighted evaluation criteria

Criteria	Weighting	Condition
Price	80%	None
Technical ability	10%	Bidders must score at least 60% of available marks
Ability to deliver on time	10%	Bidders must score at least 80% of available marks

Let's look at the example in Table 7.2. Clearly, in this case, bidders will need to focus their efforts on creating a highly competitive price. They may need to sacrifice some elements that would give a better technical ability score, but without running the risk of not achieving the pass mark. For example, they might ordinarily be tempted to demonstrate the quality of their solution by including additional training for staff. However, because price is such a critical factor in this example, unless this is a 'must-have' requirement a decision might have to be made to leave it out.

Let's look at a set of scores in this example:

Bid 1 scores 61/100 for technical ability, 80/100 for ability to deliver on time, at a price of £/€/$18,000.

Its weighted calculation is:

80/80 for price (lowest price gets full marks)
$61 \times 10\% = 6.1$ for technical ability
$90 \times 10\% = 8.0$ for ability to deliver on time
Total score = 94.1

Bid 2 scores 85/100 for technical ability, 90/100 for ability to deliver on time, at a price of £/€/$25,000.

Its weighted calculation is:

48.8/80(100 – (% variance from lowest price) × 80%)
$85 \times 10\% = 8.5$ for technical ability
$90 \times 10\% = 9.0$ for ability to deliver on time
Total score = 66.3

Here, whilst the relative quality of Bid 1 is evident in the scores achieved in the performance criteria (technical ability and ability to deliver on time), the dominance of the price criterion wiped out any advantage that these might have brought in another competition. The value of the extra quality could not be justified in this example, and the cheaper bid won.

The lesson that this example teaches us is this: if there are conditional criteria, be careful that you don't introduce unnecessary costs in order to overachieve on them. Price up the job to the required standard only, looking for added value wherever possible to give you the edge.

If, on the other hand, the quality criterion is dominant, the reverse is true: you must be sure to design a solution that will ensure that you achieve the required quality score. This might introduce cost, and you should always be cost-conscious, but try to calculate the point at which your solution balances with the given criteria, and the conditions attached.

Participating in e-auctions

In recent years, the e-auction has become an increasingly popular tool for the buyer to access the lowest price that suppliers are willing to charge. It was initially used only for commodity-type purchases (ie the bulk purchase of goods rather than services), but more and more service-related contracts are now being procured this way – much to the consternation of those selling these services.

So why do buyers use e-auctions? The reason is simple: they reduce negotiating time and cost. I have seen many figures quoted, but it seems that buyers claim to save between 5 and 25 per cent on final price by using e-auctions rather than face-to-face negotiations, and the whole process can be up to 30 per cent quicker.

How e-auctions work

In very simple terms, the e-auction process works like this: the buyer prepares the tender documents in the normal way, specifying requirements and issuing instructions to bidders about submitting their bids. As in any bid, suppliers will need to describe their solution and capability to demonstrate to the buyer that they would be able to fulfil the contract to the required standard. However, the price that it submitted is only indicative: an opening offer, if you like. The buyer will evaluate submissions against the non-price-based criteria to determine capable bidders, and will then invite shortlisted suppliers to participate in the e-auction. This is when the fun starts.

E-auction 'events' (as they are known) are actually reverse auctions, and take place over a set period of time, usually a number of hours, although I have seen longer auctions. Bidders are instructed to log into the web-based system (training is often given in advance to make sure the event runs smoothly) and are then required to make their first bid, which is recorded anonymously.

As time goes on, the idea is that bidders, who can see the offers being made by their competitors (although they are unaware which bidder is which), keep reducing their prices until the lowest offer is made. As the event ends, 'negotiations' are complete.

It sounds quite straightforward, doesn't it? However, be under no illusion, the buyer has all the power within an e-auction. Sometimes the rules state that, if you don't react to a competitor placing a lower bid within a set amount of time, you will be locked out of the rest of the process. Or the buyer might reserve the right to extend the auction at the last moment if it looks as though suppliers might be willing to keep lowering their prices.

Now it is important to understand that, as with the traditional bid evaluation model, price will not necessarily be the final deciding factor in an e-auction. The buyer may still combine your capability score with your auction offer to arrive at a decision. One of the most common misunderstandings of e-auctions is that the cheapest wins every time. As we've discussed earlier in the chapter, this is not always the case. Make sure you know what the rules are before you participate.

What happens during an e-auction

In reality, e-auctions can be very stressful! Anyone familiar with eBay will realize that all the activity takes place in the closing seconds of the event. It really does become a test of nerve as the seconds tick away and you perceive your margin to be disappearing before your eyes.

And this is the main thing to be aware of when you decide to go ahead and participate in an e-auction. Set your lowest price before the event starts, and do not be tempted to go any lower as the auction progresses. (Remember, cheapest might not win anyway!)

I have seen really experienced bid teams reduced to jelly by e-auctions, and financial directors overriding their own lowest-price decisions in the heat of the moment. To avoid all the repercussions of acting in haste, I often recommend that someone unconnected with the bid is trained on the e-auction software and is given an instruction on the lowest price he or she can enter. In this way, all of the emotion (and some of the tension) is taken out of the event.

The opinion within the bid management fraternity is one of opposition to e-auctions, since they are so heavily weighted towards the buyer. They rely on the buyer having managed the early part of the process well, with crystal-clear specifications that ensure like-for-like comparisons in the final auction. In reality, this is rarely the case (even in commodity auctions), and assumptions have to be made by the bidders that mean that the buyer does not have a completely comparable set of information. But by then it's often too late and the auction goes ahead anyway. So think carefully before committing to a bid process that will eventually end in an e-auction. You might get less than you bargained for!

SUMMARY

Pricing up your bid is one of the most important aspects of your process. Try to take out the guesswork by using the information provided by the buyer in terms of budget and evaluation criteria. Undertake continuous research on your marketplace and your competitors to ensure that your pricing strategy is sound.

Make sure your approach to pricing is flexible, and adapt your operational solution according to the precise requirements of the buyer. If the evaluation criteria are heavily weighted towards price, make sure you are not loading in extra cost that gives benefits that the buyer can't afford.

Keep asking yourself the 'big' question from Chapter 4: is it profitable? Never lose sight of why you're bidding for this contract in the first place. You don't want to win at any cost. This is especially true in e-auctions, where your profit margin diminishes as the price reduces.

Look for opportunities to add value, even in small ways. When all other factors are equal, often these small offers can be the difference between winning and losing.

Don't hide your price; introduce it as early in your bid as possible (ideally in your executive summary), alongside your value proposition, which you'll need to take time to understand fully.

The case for case studies

08

THIS CHAPTER COVERS:

- Choosing the right case studies
- How to present case studies in your bid
- What if? (Making the best of what you've got)
- References

Arguably, your past experience and successes are among your strongest sales tools, yet time after time they are underused in bids and proposals, or left out altogether. Often, a suite of generic case studies is attached as appendices to a bid or, apart from a long list of past and current clients, no reference is made to experience at all.

If you take this approach, you are expecting buyers to trust you without giving them any evidence on which to base that trust. Don't forget, buyers are doing as much as they can to avoid risk. If you don't help them to see that you are a safe and experienced supplier, they will be forced to be cautious about choosing you, especially when other bidders clearly demonstrate their track record.

Often it's your experience that is your differentiator in a bid. If others are offering an equally credible solution at a similar price, it's easy to see how the value of proven historical successes could be the winning factor in the buyer's mind.

The good news about case studies is that you can prepare them outside of the bidding process and call upon them when you need them. This is a really good discipline, and gives you some fantastic material, too, for use in your general marketing activities.

Choosing the right case studies

The first thing you need to decide is which of your case studies will be the most relevant and useful to demonstrate your capability for meeting the buyer's specific requirements. Your case studies should not merely be a general brag about your biggest, best or highest-profile customers. They are relevant stories that show that you have the right experience and can deliver for this customer.

You might actually find that you don't have a 'perfect match' case study with which to demonstrate your track record. More likely, you'll have experiences from a number of past projects that combine to show that you have the right skills and expertise. This is absolutely fine (and possibly even preferable), because it shows the diversity of your experience.

Within your executive summary outline, you'll have already identified the customer's vision and the specific challenges that this bid process needs to address. Use these as your starting point, identifying any relevant case studies that illustrate how you've met similar challenges for other customers previously. Remember, it's fine if you use a different illustration for each challenge.

Of course, most of your case study stories will be about the successful delivery of something tangible. But remember, the avoidance of something undesirable can also be very interesting to the evaluator. If you're being asked about information security, for instance, a statement that you have never had a data protection breach could be very valuable to a buyer with this as a particular concern. Or if your health and safety record is exemplary, say so in the relevant section.

How to present case studies in your bid

Your experience needs to be woven throughout your bid document. Only in exceptional circumstances should you ever attach a case study as an extra document or as an appendix. If you do this, it's less likely that it will ever get read, and the potential benefit from including it might be lost.

In my bids I use the following devices to get the experience message across. In the executive summary, I include headline information about how similar challenges have previously been met for other clients. I always quantify these successes. In the main response document, I do one of two things. I either insert 'case study notes' as call-out boxes, rather like those you see in newspapers or magazines, giving a one- or two-sentence snippet about the particular subject that is being addressed in the question. Alternatively, I include a short but complete case study to illustrate a particular piece of work. I use a template for this form of case study. It's really simple, but helps you to tell the story.

The case study template

The customer's challenge

Include here a brief description of who the customer is, and the challenge that the customer came to you for help with. If you won this piece of work through a competitive bidding process, tell the buyer. Outline the expected results, the timeframe and any other pertinent information that gives the reader some idea of the scope and scale of the task you were faced with.

The solution

This is the part of the case study where you tell the story about how you solved the problem for the customer. Think: who, what, when, where, why. Don't include any outcomes just yet. This is your description of how you designed and delivered the right solution.

Success

In this final section, describe the successes that you achieved at a high level. Show measurable outcomes, plus the tangible and intangible benefits enjoyed by the customer. If you've got a quote or a testimony from the customer, include it here. Make sure you attribute any quotes, giving a name and job title (anything anonymous just doesn't look credible).

Throughout the document I also like to insert quotes or testimonies from satisfied customers to show a more independent view of the successes achieved previously. To add extra credence to these quotes, it's a nice touch to offer to put the evaluator in touch with the customer so that the evaluator can hear the customer's testimony first-hand. (See 'References' below for more on this.)

Experience of key personnel

Another way of showing your experience is to include the details of the key individuals who will be working on the contract once it is won. Not only does this give a clear indication of the roles and responsibilities of the core team, but it also reassures the customer that those working on the contract are suitably skilled and experienced. Use the template in Table 8.1 to show the capability of your key personnel.

TABLE 8.1 Standard biography template for key individuals

Name	[Insert photo if available/appropriate]
Title	[Current job title]
Employee since	[mm/yyyy]
Role	[Brief description of the role on this contract only. The evaluator is not interested in what else this person has to do for other customers!]
Previous experience	[Brief description of past employment/roles that show relevant experience]

If you feel that individual photographs are overkill, or if you simply don't have the time or resources to obtain them all, don't worry about not including them, but if you can organize a team photograph this might be a nice touch. Remember, you're trying to show the human side of your solution here. A photograph of a motivated-looking team is a good way of trying to move the decision from logical to emotional, even in a small way.

Presenting the incumbency case study

If you are the incumbent in a bid, you have a clear and valuable different-iator – as long as you've been delivering a good service historically. (If your past performance hasn't been as strong as it could have been, have a look in the 'What if...?' section later in this chapter.) As the incumbent you have a different story to tell the evaluator compared with all of the other bidders.

Whilst other bidders will be stating the case for change, you need to remind the evaluator of the advantages of continuity. Make buyers realize that the effort (and perhaps the cost, if relevant) required on their part in extracting the contract from you and integrating it into another supplier is prohibitive and unnecessary.

To do this, try one or more of the following:

1 *Include a detailed case study of all the work you have done for the customer during the previous contracting period.* Focus particularly on set-up or transition-in activities and on any process improvements or cost reductions that you have achieved. Remind the reader of the integration between your two organizations, pointing, if you can, to any examples of true partnership that have been achieved.

The effectiveness of the incumbency case study: an example

I once included a 30-page case study in a contract renewal bid to remind a public sector customer just how much work had been done in setting up, running and improving a successful outsourcing contract since the contract was first agreed. No other bidder could demonstrate anything like this level of expertise and commitment to the customer. In the feedback session, the buyer told us that this had been a key part of the submission, reminding them of the partnership links that had been forged, the complexity of the contract, and the progress that had been made since implementation. It perfectly illustrated what was at stake in the event that a decision to move the contract should be taken. We won the contract for a further three years.

2 *Summarize all the activities carried out.* If space is at a premium and you don't want to use the long-form case study, but do want to remind the customer just what you have achieved for them during the contract lifetime, consider creating a graphic, table or timeline that gives an overview of what has been done. This can show at a glance the amount of ground that has been covered. It also implies the level of experience and expertise that is now embedded into your team for that customer. Again, this should remind the buyer just how much effort and risk would be involved in re-creating this same level of expertise in another supplier.

3 *Use photos and biographies of the people delivering the service currently.* Since your team is made up of individuals, and these are hopefully well known to your customer, then use this fact to your advantage by including brief biographies of the key people engaged in delivering the contract. The purpose of this is to reassure the evaluators that this team is experienced and knowledgeable. What is more, they are available and already doing the job right now. (Don't forget, other bidders may show possible candidates for key positions in their bids, but often can't guarantee their availability – you can.) Use the template in Table 8.2 (note that it differs slightly from Table 8.1). It will remind the customer what each individual is already doing for them and what the individual has achieved on behalf of the customer to date. But it will also demonstrate individuals' wider experience and why you chose them to be in the team in the first place.

4 *Use snippets of the larger case study.* Even if you decide to include a long-form case study in your bid submission, it is also good practice to include snippets of the same case study within the main response document to continually remind readers of your experience for them.

TABLE 8.2   Biography template for key individuals in a bid where you are the incumbent

Name	[Insert photo]
Title	[Current job title]
Worked on contract for [customer] since	[mm/yyyy]
Role	[Brief description of role on this contract only. The evaluator is not interested in what else this person has to do for other customers!]
Previous experience	[Brief description of past employment/roles that show relevant experience]
Highlights to date on contract xx	[One or two examples of quantifiable successes achieved for the customer to date in the delivery of this contract]

Include these in the form of case study notes or call-out boxes. Always show demonstrable and quantifiable successes.

5 *Include other case studies.* It's tempting to focus all your attention on the work you've done for this customer, but remember that the broader your experience, the easier the decision for the evaluator. So include other relevant case study stories as well as the one you're rebidding for.

6 *Refer to PR or awards successes.* If, during the lifetime of the contract, you have publicized the contract and its successes through PR, then show the outputs in your renewal bid. If you've helped buyers to promote their own expertise and successful partnership management, this will be another point in your favour. Similarly, if you've entered the piece of work for an award and have been shortlisted or have won, remind them of this fact too. It all helps to show how strong the relationship is, and how there are added value benefits on top of the ongoing delivery of the job in hand.

Avoiding conflicts of interest

Of course, choosing the right case studies is vital if you're going to get the right messages across. You must pick your most relevant examples, remembering that it's fine to use component parts of a whole story to build up a demonstrable capability message. But a note of caution here: think carefully about the information you're giving away about your existing customers. There are a couple of aspects to this decision.

First, is your existing customer in competition with your prospect in any way? If so, they might not wish you to share their case study in this instance. Clearly you don't want to upset an existing customer in order to win a new one. Don't overlook this potential conflict of interest. If necessary, don't use this case study at all, even if it's your closest fit. Go back to other stories and build up a capability story from them instead.

Second, are your existing customers happy to share their 'secrets'? Often, as a supplier you will have helped to solve a problem or a challenge for your customer, and it's natural to want to show this in your case studies. However, the customer may not be quite so happy to admit to needing help in the first place. But then again, they might be more than content to demonstrate that they are creative in solving problems and therefore outsource to experts to get the job done well. Instead of trying to guess how your existing customer might feel, if there's any doubt talk to them and ask for permission to include the case study in your bid. If necessary, show them the text you are proposing to use and get their express permission.

When you take this route, always state in your bid document that you have obtained the permission of the existing customer to include the case study. It gives a strong and important message that you care about customer confidentiality. This is always a good thing in the eyes of prospective buyers, who then know to expect the same level of protection for their information in the future.

Confidentiality of case study information

When requesting permission to use a case study in your bid, remember that in the private sector your bid should be being conducted in a confidential environment. Most B2B bid processes commence with the signing of a mutual confidentiality agreement or non-disclosure agreement. This ensures that information cannot be passed on or shared with third parties. In such cases, then, you can reassure your customers that any sensitive information will be safe and will be seen only by the prospect.

In the public sector, however, it is possible that the content of your bid could be made public under a freedom of information request. In such cases, you could request that case studies are treated as sensitive material to protect your customers' confidentiality (see Chapter 10 for further details on how to do this). However, this may not be accepted. It's best to check with the buyer first, asking how such a request is likely to be viewed. Depending on the response, you'll then need to take an appropriate decision about whether to include the information or not.

If you later wish to use the case studies you have prepared as part of your general marketing activities, make sure that you get full permission from your customer before releasing any information into the public domain.

The anonymous case study

Of course, there is one way around the issue of protecting existing customers, and that is not to identify them by name in the case study. You could identify an existing customer by naming the customer as 'Customer A' or by using a description: 'a local authority' or 'an accountancy practice'. This doesn't necessarily weaken your story. Make it clear that you are doing this to protect your customer's confidentiality. Again, this is a positive message about how you treat your customers and an implied promise to the buyer that the same courtesy will be extended to them.

What if? (Making the best of what you've got)

Earlier in this chapter, we looked at what to do if you don't have a parallel story to use that can show that you have the right experience. We also looked at the potential conflict of interest that can arise when using existing customers to demonstrate past performance. But there are a couple of other problems that can crop up when it comes to using case studies.

What if the customer knows your weaknesses?

It might be that you've worked with this customer before and didn't perform as well as either you or they would have liked. Or you might believe that competitors are trying to knock your reputation, highlighting their perception of your weaknesses to the buyer. Whatever the reason, there may be a time when you have to admit that you haven't had a perfect track record in the past. This is only a problem if nothing has changed in your operating model and buyers might perceive that the same problems might well occur again if they selected you.

So the rule is this: admit to the problems; don't pretend they don't exist. However, alongside this, you also need to demonstrate clearly how you've addressed those problems, adapted your way of working and learnt from the experience. Only if you can show the buyer that the shortcomings could never happen again will you present a convincing case.

What if you don't have any experience?

If you're bidding to deliver something you've no experience of, or are entering a brand new marketplace in which you have no track record, think carefully first. If all the other bidders are in the same boat (perhaps the customer wants a new partner in a brand new initiative that has never been tried before), then your lack of relevant experience will not put you at a disadvantage against others. (You might need to be wary of the risks involved in such a project, but that's a whole other consideration.)

The problem comes when others have a clear track record to refer to and you do not. As a new entrant, you could use the experience gained by individual employees in past positions or projects and draw them all together to show a collective expertise. However, you really do need to see things from the buyer's perspective in this scenario. Would you be convinced that this wasn't a risky option? Would you want your supplier to gain their experience in this field on your project? Be really objective here. If you can't convince yourself, you'll never convince a buyer. Consider not bidding this time, getting the experience elsewhere and then coming back to opportunities like this one in the future.

What if the bid requires key personnel to be identified, but you can't be sure who'll be available?

Of course, wherever possible, you should plan to put the best people in your solution and therefore your bid. You are much more likely to win with your most skilled and experienced team. But sometimes you won't be able to do this.

You might need to recruit for new staff in order to deliver the proposed solution. If this is the case, then you will need to indicate the required standards against which you will recruit, rather than naming an individual. It would also be useful to include some information about how you'd go about the recruitment process, to reassure the buyer. Even better, you could offer to involve the buyer in the later stages of your selection process (but only if you're happy for this level of involvement!).

Or, if timings are uncertain, you might not be able to guarantee the availability of your preferred individuals, who may (or may not) be busy on other projects at the time the contract is agreed. If this is genuinely the case, I advise that you include your 'A' team in the bid, clearly indicating that you would replace them with individuals of similar skill levels in the event that any one of them is unavailable. I would never advise including your best people in a bid if you've no intention of putting them on the delivery team. This 'bait and switch' approach could be potentially damaging to your fledgling relationship with your customer and can quickly earn you the wrong kind of reputation.

References

Whom to ask, how and when

In almost every bid I have ever worked on, there has been a request to provide references. In the unlikely event that you are not asked to provide them, I advise that you volunteer at least two anyway. This will show the evaluator that you are confident that your existing customers will speak positively about their experiences of working with you as a supplier.

If, therefore, you are always going to need to provide references, who should you choose, and how should you manage this process?

In my opinion, the best people to provide references are those customers whose case studies you have used within your bid submission. This is a neat tie-in, and offers the evaluator the chance to find out directly that what you've said can be substantiated by your customer. Of course, if you've had to put forward any anonymous case studies, you won't be able to use these as reference points, for obvious reasons.

If you are the incumbent, you are often not allowed to nominate the contract in hand as a reference point, so you'll need to provide the most suitable alternative.

The factors to take into consideration when deciding which references to nominate are:

- Similarity of service – will it enable the evaluator to ascertain that you could do this job?

- Current performance – are you performing well at the moment for this customer? Would the customer say the right kinds of things about you?

- Reference fatigue – how many times have you asked a customer to act as a reference for you already? Try to spread around the favours you ask from existing customers.

- Conflict of interest – is there any reason that providing a reference to your prospective customer might put the existing customer in a difficult position (for example, if they're competitors)?

I do recommend that you ask your existing customers for permission to include them as a reference point in your bid. (Do this as early as possible in the process – just in case they have an objection.) They won't always be contacted by the prospect, but it's better that they know in advance that there is a possibility that they will be.

If you've a good enough relationship with your references, ask them to let you know when they have been contacted by the prospect. Try to find out what they were asked. Often, the content of the reference call/e-mail can give you an idea of the concerns or risks that the buyer is trying to assess. You might be able to work this knowledge back into your final presentation or into any clarification process that is still ongoing.

SUMMARY

Case studies are a great tool for demonstrating your experience and expertise, and you should always include them in some shape or form in your submission. Spend time considering which case studies you are going to use to substantiate your capability claims. Weave your experience throughout the document – don't hide it in an appendices section at the back.

Present your stories carefully, ensuring they demonstrate not only what you have done, but how well you did it. Remember, you're trying to reassure the buyer that you can deliver for them successfully – as you've done before. If you are the incumbent, you should have a massive advantage. Decide how best to exploit this.

Always offer references, even if you're not specifically asked to. Choose carefully and communicate with those you've nominated, both before and after references are taken up.

It's good to talk

09

Influencing and persuading throughout the process

THIS CHAPTER COVERS:

- Understanding your starting position
- Building understanding and influencing the buyer and other stakeholder groups
- The face-to-face session: preparing for the final presentation

---

Much of this book has been concerned with the planning for and creation of the written submission in the bidding process. But, however good your written submission, it's unlikely that you'll ever win a bid competition without some level of dialogue with the customer. In this chapter we look at the importance of building a relationship with key stakeholders within the customer's organization before, during and after the bidding process. If you can build trust, understanding and mutual respect, you're going to be in a strong position when the evaluation phase is under way.

Of course, much depends on how well you know a customer, and how strong the links are between your two organizations. I would always recommend a multi-contact strategy when building links with a customer or prospect. The more key people your team knows within an organization, the better your insight will be and the greater your influence. If there's only a single point of contact between two key people, there's always a risk of your relationship disappearing if one of them moves on.

Understanding your starting position

During a bidding process, it's your relationship with the buyer that is critical to the eventual outcome. You need to keep the buyer, as the gatekeeper to and major influencer of the rest of the decision-making group, on your side. In most cases, the buyer will recommend a preferred supplier to the other decision makers at the end of the process, so it's vital that you are seen to be a compliant and enthusiastic participant, willing to play by the buyer's rules. You will still need a strategy whereby you and your team influence and persuade other key stakeholders involved in the process, but let's look at the state of your relationship with the prospect. You're likely to be in one of three situations.

1. You are proactively developing a relationship with the prospect

Of course, if you don't already have a relationship with an organization, there is no fixed process that I can give you that will work every time to create one. But you will need to be targeted and focused on creating and developing a relationship. Do your research on the prospect's vision, strategy and challenges and begin to work out what you might offer that will help to achieve them in some small (or large!) way. You'll need to work out a route into the organization, with a view ultimately to finding out who it is that is in charge of procurement. This in itself could be a challenging process but, if you have someone in your organization in charge of sales, this type of activity should not be unfamiliar to him or her.

The objective is to build sufficient awareness within your target organization of what you can do and to start to create an interest in your particular offering. This may be outside any immediate need the customer has. If the target organization has a preferred or approved supplier list, then your aim will be to make it into this group. If they don't, you will probably have to invest time and resources in this phase, maybe even offering to undertake a small project on a no-cost basis to prove yourself. Or you might persuade your contact(s) to come and visit you or one of your customers, and see for themselves the good work you're already producing. However you choose to do it, buyers need to be clear about your capability and your differentiators at the point at which they are commencing a buying cycle.

The key to gaining new customers via the proactive route is patience. Products and services purchased via tender processes can have a very long sales cycle. As part of your research, try to identify where the buyer is in the current cycle and act accordingly. Ideally, your patience will pay off and, at the point at which the buyer moves into the active part of the cycle, you will be at the front of the buyer's mind and possibly even setting the standard. Sometimes this will mean that an opportunity doesn't go out to tender at all, or that you end up helping to shape the ITT.

2. You're already a supplier or have been recommended or approved to supply

In the ideal scenario, your relationship will have started way before the tender documents were ever published. You might have supplied the customer before, or you might have been introduced or recommended by someone in your network. You might have been through some kind of supplier approval process with this organization. Regardless of how your relationship began, your long-term aim should be to build trust and a two-way understanding with a view to winning new business. Even if you're on an approved supplier list, you'll still need to be proactive and remind the buyer about any innovations, successes or good news that elevate you above the others that have been pre-selected. In this way, when the buyer does have a contract to put out to the market, you will be in a strong position.

This doesn't always mean that the buyer won't put the contract out to tender. Buyers might prefer (or be obliged) to run a competitive bid process to ensure that they are getting the best that the market can offer, rather than negotiating solely with you. Don't take offence at this decision. Instead, offer to assist in the creation of the ITT, giving advice on the kinds of questions that will help the buyer to identify the best-match supplier (that'll be you, then). Then, once the ITT is published, use your knowledge and understanding of the customer's vision and challenges to put forward a totally customer-focused bid.

3. You don't have an existing relationship with the prospect

You might have identified a contract opportunity from a public register and have now decided to bid for it. There will also be occasions when your generic marketing pays off, and a buyer that you don't know approaches you with an opportunity for which they would like you to bid. Either way, you are starting your relationship from scratch at the beginning of the bid process. Clearly this is not ideal, and you will have to work fast and well in order to get this right.

The best way is to initiate dialogue with the buyer and other stakeholders in order to obtain further information about the challenges and requirements of the invitation to tender; we'll look at this in more detail in a moment. Do look for opportunities to get in front of the buyer, and take them when they arise. If you are unknown to the buyer, be sure that your written submission is created in sufficient detail to create a really good understanding of your offering. Use plenty of case studies and offer references even if not asked. Prepare really well for any site visit or presentation. There might be other suppliers who are, on paper, ahead of you in the competition, but I do believe that this ground can be made up with a well-planned campaign.

Building understanding and influencing the buyer and other stakeholder groups

However you came by the opportunity, as you work towards creating your bid submission documents you'll need to be as certain as you can that you're on the right lines.

Often suppliers think that you can't or shouldn't ask for any further information once you have received a tender document from a buyer. I don't agree. I believe that a good buyer will be receptive to questions and requests for clarification from bidders. After all, it's in their interest to be sure that you are submitting a bid that meets their requirements as closely as possible.

Do, however, consider carefully what you are asking the buyer. If it's clear that you haven't read the document thoroughly and you are asking for information that has already been provided, the buyer will be unimpressed.

Even in tightly managed public sector bids, there should always be access to the buyer, although you might have to conduct your discussions in writing. Don't let this put you off. Similarly, don't worry that questions you ask might be shared with other bidders. You need to be sure that you have all the information that *you* need, so go ahead and ask. The buyer will share your questions (as they will in most private sector bids too), but will be aware of who asked what. So, if you're asking all the right questions and leading the thought processes of the other bidders, the buyer will see that this is the case.

If available to you, try to obtain access to end-users of your service or product. Bear in mind that, in a public sector bid, any informal access to end-users is closed to you, but you might be able to request this via formal channels. If you do get in front of end-users, try to find out as much as possible about the everyday challenges that they face and build this understanding into your bid. It's likely that someone representing end-users will be involved in the evaluation and selection decision. If you can demonstrate to this group that you understand their needs and are planning to address known challenges, you are much more likely to get their vote!

In addition, try to set up conversations between senior members of your team and the prospect's leadership team so that the highest-level strategies and challenges can be understood and addressed.

A word of caution, here, however: be aware of any rules that the buyer has stipulated about contact during the bidding process. This applies equally in the public and private sectors. Keep the buyer informed about any conversations with stakeholder groups that you might initiate. Offer to document these discussions so that they can be shared with other bidders. Avoid anything that could be misinterpreted as bribery or an attempt to exert undue influence! Basically, show the buyer that you're keen to create the right solution, but equally keen to stick to the rules.

Supplier briefings

Sometimes the buyer will call a supplier briefing session shortly after issuing the tender documents. This is most common in the public sector, but not unheard of in the private sector. At this session, the buyer will brief suppliers on the contract requirements as well as reminding them about the instructions they should follow.

These are not-to-be-missed sessions that can reveal an awful lot about who else is bidding for the contract and how they are tackling the process. You can also pick up vital clues about the buyer's preferences and unwritten requirements at these sessions. Look at body language and listen to the subtext of the discussions as well as the official briefing. Even if you feel well informed about the opportunity and the requirements and instructions, always attend a supplier briefing if invited. If you don't attend, you might give the impression that you're not that interested in participating in the process – not really the message you're trying to convey.

After the bid is submitted

Once you've submitted your bid, keep the dialogue going with the buyer. Check that the document arrived safely and that any electronic versions are working properly. Even if you submitted your bid via an e-procurement site, I would still recommend a quick call to check that all is as it should be with your submission.

Be responsive if there are any questions or clarifications forthcoming from the buyer during the evaluation period. If you are asked only for verbal clarification, always provide written confirmation of the information you have given, even if only by e-mail. At this stage, all you can do is show your ongoing appetite for winning, and your willingness to provide any additional information required.

After that, sometimes it will go quiet for a while as the evaluation panel reads all the documents and meets to compare notes. One of two things is likely to happen next. The buyer will make an announcement about the winning bid or will call suppliers to make a presentation or host a site visit – or both. (Actually, there is a third possibility. That is that the buyer suspends or even withdraws the process. This might happen for a number of reasons: perhaps there never was a contract to award, and this has been a benchmarking exercise. Alternatively, buyers might now realize that the process has not provided any bids of the right quality or within the budget range. They might even realize that outsourcing their contract in this way would not be right for their company after all. If this is the case, try to find out why the process is halted and chalk this one up to experience.)

If you are invited to participate in the final stage of a process, well done! You've made it this far, but to close the deal and win you've got one more very important task to complete.

The face-to-face session: preparing for the final presentation

By this stage, you'll probably be one of the last two or three suppliers left in the bidding process, since it would be too time-consuming for the evaluation panel to accommodate any more than this number. It's tempting to think that, if you're down to the last two, there's now a 50:50 chance of winning. However, by this stage, the evaluation is likely to favour one bidder over the other or others.

You may be the supplier in pole position, in which case a defensive approach is needed to help you to protect your lead. Or you may be at the back of the starting grid, in which case you'll need an attacking approach that can help to remedy any perceived shortcomings that have arisen from your written submission. In reality, you're unlikely to know where you sit in the rankings going into the final presentation stage, although you might have received some clues or hints from your buyer or someone else acting as 'coach' or friend from within the buying organization. You'll need to take this stage very seriously and give it everything you've got. Whatever happens, you've got to outdo the competition during this stage.

Here's my preparation checklist for your final presentation session (if you're required to host a site visit rather than make a presentation, most of the advice shown here will still be relevant, but check the section below this one as well):

1 *Prepare early.* There might not be much time between the submission of the written bid and the call to attend the presentation. To be on the safe side, don't wait to be called; start your preparation as soon as you've submitted your written bid, whilst everything is still fresh in your team's mind. Start creating your presentation theme and sketch out the slides. Use your executive summary as the starting point; this presentation has to be totally customer-focused, and the main themes you need should be here.

2 *Check your instructions.* As soon as you have confirmation that you're required to make a final presentation, look carefully at the customer's instructions for the session. They may well dictate how many people can attend, how long the session will be, what agenda items they'd like covered, the format of the presentation, and the like. As you did with the original tender instructions, make sure you read them thoroughly and understand them completely. Check with the buyer if there's any doubt about what's expected of you.

3 *Select your team.* You'll next need to decide who is going to make the all-important presentation. When selecting the team, look at who will be attending from the evaluation team as well as the agenda items you need to cover. Your team will need to be able to confidently and convincingly present as well as responding to any questions posed by the evaluation team. So, if they're sending along an IT expert, for instance, it might be worth considering matching that person with

an IT expert of your own. Try to avoid the 'beauty parade' approach, that is, sending senior people who don't have a complete grasp on the bid, just to impress the customer. Everyone in the team must have a role and must be there for a very good reason. Work out presentation roles and responsibilities and share them amongst selected team members. Everyone at the presentation must know the bid inside out, so the first requirement is that they've all read the bid document and are familiar with it. If the customer has dictated a set number of people, certain team members might need to cover a topic that is outside their normal remit. It goes without saying that they will need additional support from subject-matter experts during the preparation phase, and possibly extra rehearsal time.

4 *Refine your presentation.* Now that you have them, refine the presentation according to the instructions you've been given. Follow them closely; if they require you to show how you are going to deliver the solution, then concentrate on presenting the benefits of your solution alongside its features. But the main thing to remember when preparing your presentation is the fact that you're trying to convince the buyer to select you over the other remaining bidder(s). Assuming those left will all be able to deliver a compliant solution, other than price, what will be the differentiator? The panel will be looking, either consciously or unconsciously, for something that sets one bidder apart from the others. Go back to your executive summary and be sure to expand now on your bid theme, your recognition of the customer's vision and challenges, and the tangible and intangible benefits that you outlined there.

5 *Rehearse.* Since your presentation will almost certainly be time-limited, it needs to be carefully constructed and rehearsed. If it isn't, I can almost guarantee that it will overrun and key messages will be left out. It doesn't matter if everyone on the team isn't a highly polished, expert presenter. But if you don't practise, it will show, and you run the risk of what you're saying being drowned out by the way you're saying it. There seems to be a universal reluctance to rehearse presentations, for a myriad of reasons. But once you've persuaded your team, and they've got through the first rehearsal (which will be awful, I can almost promise – but that would have been how it would have sounded to the customer...), and the second (which will be a bit better, but still too long and with bits missed out), the third will start to feel comfortable. By this stage, you can begin to polish

the content, and your team's natural expertise and passion for the job they're describing will start to show through. In addition, any technical glitches will be ironed out, the temptation just to read the slides will have been overcome, and each presenter will be comfortable and familiar with the pace and timing of the overall pitch.

6 *Anticipate difficult questions.* You're not quite ready for the big day yet, though. There will almost certainly be a question-and-answer (Q&A) item on the agenda: the undoing of many a polished and rehearsed presentation. As uncomfortable as it might be, you need to prepare for every possible question, including the worst questions that the customer could possibly ask. You'll probably know, deep down, what these questions are. Up until now you've probably managed to avoid tackling them, but I'm afraid that's no longer an option. As a group, agree not only how you're going to answer, if asked, but also exactly who is going to answer. This holds true for all the questions you anticipate being asked, not just the difficult ones. My recommendation is that you have a Q&A chairperson, even if you don't announce the fact to the customer. When any questions are asked, the chair will direct the question to the appropriate owner (as agreed during your rehearsals), who will answer. At this stage it's vital that everyone understands that *only that person* will speak in relation to the given topic. Chipping in or adding to a response is not permitted; it undermines the respondent and gives the impression of a fragmented team. Enforce this rule during rehearsals (yes, you need to practise answering tough questions too) to ensure that this very final part of your strategy goes to plan.

7 *On the day.* On the day itself, try to ensure that you and your team are as stress-free as possible. This might mean that no one schedules in any meetings before the presentation that might overrun or that might distract them from the day's most important activity. It definitely means travelling with plenty of time to spare, giving everyone time to freshen up and to set up and check equipment beforehand.

Other tips for presentation day include:

- Make sure you get the dress code right. Match the style of the customer. Check with the customer if there's any uncertainty.

- Have a back-up plan in case of laptop failure, projector incompatibility or any other technical hitch. Old-fashioned printed copies are a good bet as an absolutely failsafe option.

- Check the customer's preference for leave-behinds (a copy of the slide pack, for example).
- Bring a copy of your bid document with you, just in case you need to refer to it during the session.
- Nominate one person as note taker, and have him or her document any points for clarification so that nothing gets forgotten.
- Relax and try to enjoy it!

Hosting site visits as part of the final stage

Sometimes you'll be required to host a site visit instead of, or as well as, giving a presentation. Broadly speaking, I suggest that you follow my advice on presentations when preparing for such an event. There are, however, a few additional things to bear in mind:

- Little touches like reserved parking spaces by the door, a welcome sign and a fully briefed receptionist are a great start – or you could be waiting to greet them in person as they arrive. Treat your visitors like VIPs: good coffee, the best biscuits! Oh, and have a tidy-up before they arrive.

- As they move round your premises, the panel are likely to come into contact with people from your organization who are not directly involved in the opportunity. Make sure everyone knows who the guests are and why they are visiting today. Try to ensure a positive and accommodating response to any questions asked.

- Be prepared to show your evaluators any part of your premises or operation – don't be defensive. Treat the visit like a quality-control inspection or an audit. Obviously, if there is any danger of a breach of confidentiality or information security, be aware and take appropriate action. Just be sure to explain what you are doing and why.

- At the end of the visit, offer to leave the evaluators in a private meeting room so that they can discuss their observations and identify any outstanding points of clarification.

And finally, if there have been any matters that require clarification during the presentation session or site visit, follow them up immediately and report back to the evaluation panel in writing as soon as is practical. Even if there are none, write to the buyer after the session, thanking him or her for the time, and asking if there are any outstanding matters that require clarification. If not, then your work is done. All you can now do is wait.

SUMMARY

Aim to develop and build a good relationship with not only the buyer but also key stakeholders in your target organization. The earlier you do this and the broader the links, the better.

Closely observe the rules of engagement during a live bid process, making sure you take advantage of any legitimate opportunity to discuss, clarify and otherwise show your enthusiasm and interest in this opportunity. Then, after the bid is submitted, be responsive to requests for clarification.

Begin your preparation for the presentation and/or site visit stage as soon as possible – ideally straight after you submit your written documents. As soon as you receive notification that you are required to present or host a site visit, choose your team, choose your messages and draw up a rehearsal schedule. Prepare fully for this final test. Whatever happens, you have to be better than your competitors. Don't leave anything to chance. Rehearse, rehearse and then rehearse some more.

And the winner is...
(What happens after the decision is made)

10

THIS CHAPTER COVERS:

- How winners and losers are notified
- Learning lessons for future bids
- Creating a knowledge base for future bids
- Measuring your bid performance over time

There's much debate in the bid world about what rate of success you should expect to achieve. There's one school of thought that says, since most competitions include about five suppliers at the shortlist stage, the average win rate must be one in five, or 20 per cent. I'm not sure I agree with this, since it assumes a level playing field every time, and that eventually you will get lucky just by the law of averages. I believe that, if you apply the techniques and good practice described in this book, you can expect to win at least 50 per cent of the bids you enter, versus something nearer 10 per cent without. But of course there are never any guarantees, and much depends on the particular set of circumstances you are in. We'll look at win rates in more detail a little later in this chapter.

Eventually, then, the time will come when you receive the decision from the buyer. Assuming that they decide to proceed with awarding the contract, it will, of course, go one of two ways for you. Either you'll win or you won't. So it'll either be a time for celebration or be a learning opportunity (let's try to be positive about this).

Actually, whatever the outcome, this bid is not quite over yet. Win or lose, you'll have learnt a tremendous amount along the way, and it's vital that you use these experiences for the next bid that you decide to enter.

But before we move on to the lessons learnt stage, let's just have a look at what you can expect to happen after the buyer has made the decision. How will you find out whether you've won or not?

How winners and losers are notified

In the private sector

Buyers will most probably begin by notifying their first-choice supplier that it has 'won'. At this stage there might be some last-minute price negotiations requested, or buyers might attach some conditions to the offer and request to undertake some form of due diligence or audit. They might make the offer 'subject to contract' and commence legal negotiations. Or they might just congratulate you and tell you that the order's on its way.

Because there are no hard-and-fast rules about how a deal must be concluded in this sector, it's not really possible to give a clear indication of what to expect at this stage. On larger contracts, however, where terms are negotiable, it's definitely a good idea to get legal representation to ensure that the contract is not unduly weighted against you. For smaller contracts, where you've seen the buyer's standard terms and conditions during the bid process and are happy to accept them, this stage can be relatively short and not too difficult to navigate.

While these discussions are ongoing with the winner, buyers often do not tell the other bidders that an offer has been made. Instead, they will transmit a holding message, advising that the decision process is still under way. You can see why buyers would want to do this: in case talks break down with the preferred supplier, there are then a number of other willing suppliers waiting patiently in the wings. If you are experiencing a delay in receiving a decision from the buyer, and seem to be being held at arm's length, this could be the reason. There's really not much you can do at this stage, I'm afraid, except wait until you eventually receive your call (actually it'll probably be an e-mail or letter – in my experience, buyers avoid those awkward thanks-but-no-thanks conversations).

When you do receive it, it will probably tell you that you came a close second. In private sector competitions, there is a standing joke amongst bid managers: that buyers tell every unsuccessful bidder that it was very close, but that the winner was just ahead. They normally tell you that you lost on price too – again, the easiest option, the one that will readily be accepted by most bidders and that needs little additional explanation.

It's also worth knowing that there's a third possible outcome in the private sector: the buyer simply does not proceed to award. This might happen for a number of reasons: the buyer cannot find a suitable supplier or the right deal; circumstances within the organization have changed, and the need to outsource no longer exists; or the tender was only ever a benchmarking exercise to provide market insight.

Whatever the reason for not proceeding, this can be a frustrating time for bidders, as they wait and wait for a decision that is continually put back by the buyer. Sometimes you will eventually get the buyer to admit that the opportunity is now closed and will not be awarded. Other times, the buyer will never actually formally notify you of the conclusion of the bid process, and you're forced to arrive yourself at the conclusion that there is not going to be an award this time. This is the worst, most frustrating outcome of a bid process, and I think it's poor practice on the part of buyers to leave bidders without a swift and conclusive decision. There's nothing that can be done about this, but it's worth knowing that it is a possible outcome before you start. If you're invited to tender by the same buyer in the future, it should be a consideration in the 'winnable' aspect of your decision to bid (as discussed in Chapter 4).

In the public sector

The good news in the public sector is that, unless there are exceptional circumstances, an award will definitely be made each time, although it is worth noting that it is not unknown for the decision to be delayed!

Above-threshold tenders

Assuming your bid is above the relevant *OJEU* threshold and is being conducted under the EU regulations, then buyers will have to notify all bidders of the final decision on the same day. This formal notification is known as an 'award decision notice', and it must include certain information. Firstly, it should advise the identity of the winning bidder(s); there may be more than one successful bidder, depending on the terms of the original notice. It should also inform of the award criteria and reasons for the decision. The regulations state that, 'if practicable', you will also receive information about your own score and how you scored versus the winning bidder (if you are unsuccessful). In due course, notice of award should also be published in *OJEU*.

Remedies Directive for unsuccessful bidders

Since 2009, the regulations have been amended to include a Remedies Directive to protect suppliers from poor procurement practice – most notably from the practice of direct awards (where buyers award contracts without engaging the market in open competition). The Remedies Directive helps suppliers in three ways:

1 It ensures that bidders receive the right information in the award decision notice (as described above), giving them transparency about why they were successful or unsuccessful in the process.

2 It mandates a 'standstill period' of 10 days, during which unsuccessful bidders can mount a legal challenge to the process (of which more below).

3 It introduces much tougher sanctions against authorities that do not follow the processes set out in the regulations. In the past, the only possible remedy for suppliers was a claim for damages, post-award. Now, suppliers may be able to halt the contract going ahead at all if they can prove to the courts, before the contract commences, the contracting authority's ineffectiveness in the procurement process. If the contract has already begun, the courts may declare the award ineffective and fine the authority; damages may also be awarded to other affected parties.

If you believe that the contracting authority has a case to answer, you will need to act fast – ideally within the standstill period. However, under the Remedies Directive, you can still bring a case within three months of the award being made, especially if you could not have known about the breach at the time it was originally made and it only subsequently comes to light.

If you do feel that you have grounds to mount a legal challenge, you will most definitely need specialist legal advice. As with any legal proceedings, you'll need to think very carefully before you commence this action. Realistically, there are only three grounds for bringing a case. These are:

1 that the *OJEU* notice was not publicized correctly;

2 that the contract was finalized within the standstill period;

3 that the mini-tendering rules were not observed in a framework agreement.

Even if you are certain that you have a good case, be aware that the costs will be considerable, as will the time, resources and energy required to mount the challenge; and, of course, the outcome will be uncertain. Since the directive is relatively new, there is little case law upon which to draw at the moment.

Below-threshold tenders

For under-threshold contracts, the standstill period does not apply, nor does the obligation to notify the other bidders of their relative performances versus the winner. Instead, the process is much more akin to that in the private sector. The buyer will notify the preferred supplier first and, once everything is agreed, will then notify the other bidders to tell them that they have been unsuccessful this time. This doesn't mean that you can't ask for feedback, and I would always recommend that you do.

The winning public sector bidder – what happens next?

If you're the winning supplier in an above-threshold award, the 10 days of the standstill period can be an anxious time as you wait to see whether any other bidder starts proceedings. But this is rare, and in the vast majority of cases nothing at all happens during this period. Typically, after the 10 days are over, the terms of the final contract are agreed and the contract signed. For agreements of this size, it's a good idea to have legal representation at the final contract negotiation stage, to make sure that you are fully aware of your obligations and that they are not unduly onerous.

For smaller, below-threshold awards, there may be final agreement on the specification of the actual work you will be carrying out, and a simple contract to sign. You might also need to wait for the authority to raise a purchase order before the work can commence.

And then, in all cases, the hard work of delivering the contract can begin.

Learning lessons for future bids

Your bidding experiences are invaluable for ensuring that you improve your chances of success with each new competition you enter into. View each process as a learning opportunity, and take time to consider what you might do differently next time.

Even if you won this time, just be mindful of the fact that your competition might be getting themselves into better shape for the next competition. Don't stand still and let them get ahead of you.

If you were not successful this time, be sure that you have learnt from both internal and external feedback so that you're in better shape for the next attempt! In addition, make a point of recording the date of the expiry of the contract in your diary. In good time before the renewal date, re-establish contact with the buyer to make sure you'll be in the running again the next time the contract comes around.

So how should you go about learning lessons from your bidding experiences? Below is some guidance about how to collect useful information and to analyse it.

Review your own performance

Once you've finished with the celebrations or commiserations, take time to conduct an internal review of the bid process that you've just completed. It need be no more than a simple session in which all your bid contributors identify what went well and what didn't go well. Ask them for constructive feedback about how things could be improved in the future, and agree a way of working for future competitions. If it's available, share the buyer's feedback with the team (see below for how to go about obtaining this) so that everyone is aware of the areas that might need more focus next time.

Set up an action plan to address any areas of specific weakness straight away. Don't wait until the next ITT arrives before working on your quality management system, or your sustainability policy, or whichever area in which you didn't score full marks.

Seek detailed feedback from the buyer

Whether you've won or lost, immediately after you've received the decision from the buyer ask for a debrief. If you're the winner, you might think this is a waste of time, especially when you might be moving straight into the business of delivering the contract. However, it's as important to know why your bid was selected above others, and the only way you will truly know this is by asking for feedback.

Private sector feedback

In the private sector you probably won't get much back: maybe a very high-level outline of the reasons you did or didn't win. If you are one of the losing bidders, almost every time you will be told that price played a part. To be honest, I sometimes think that buyers simply give this reason because it's the easiest: the one that bidders will most readily accept. Just occasionally, however, you will find a buyer that is willing to give you a more detailed appraisal of your performance. Because you definitely won't get it if you don't, always ask. It'll be worth it on those occasions when you do get the feedback.

Public sector feedback

In the public sector, if any contract is subject to the standstill period ruling the buyer will also be obliged to provide you with a debrief, although this obligation is time-limited (you normally have to ask within the 10 days). Make sure you ask straight away – don't miss out on this opportunity to gather vital information on not only your own strengths and weaknesses but also possibly those of other bidders.

Often, within the public sector, buyers will have their own template for providing feedback. Check whether this is the case when you request the debrief. If they don't, you'll need to set out a specific set of questions that buyers can respond to.

How to structure your feedback request (all cases)

Of course, the feedback that you request will be determined by the process you followed and the submission you were required to produce. I would recommend that you keep your request as brief as possible, focusing on the core aspects of the bid in question and not asking for feedback on too many separate points. (This might result in the buyer declining the whole request.)

Always put your request in writing, and send it to the procurement lead who originally sent you the tendering documents. Make sure that you provide contact information in order for the buyer to return feedback to you easily.

The following list of questions is just a sample selection but should give you a pretty good starting point for your debrief request. As indicated above, I wouldn't recommend asking all of these questions each time; that would be very onerous for the buyer and might put them off giving any feedback at all. Alternatively, you might wish to consider focusing your questions on the actual solution you proposed, rather than the bidding process.

On the format/content of the bid

1 How well did we follow your instructions?

2 Was all the content relevant and useful? How well did it meet your specification?

3 Did you find it easy to read?

4 Overall, was the information provided too long, too short or about right?

5 How could we have improved our bid document?

6 How well did we demonstrate our understanding of your requirements and challenges?

7 How easy was it to grasp what we were proposing?

8 Did we address any concerns you had about delivery or transition risk (from the existing supplier)?

9 Would you have liked to see more or less information about our past experience (case studies)?

10 What were the principal characteristics of the winning bid, compared with those that were unsuccessful?

Pricing proposal

11 How did our price compare with other bids?

12 Did we demonstrate the value of our proposition clearly enough?

Presentation and follow-up (if applicable)

13 How could our presentation have been improved?

In general

14 Overall, was our level of engagement with you too little, too much or about right during this process?

15 Are there any other observations or comments to help us improve our future engagement with your organization?

Using the Freedom of Information (FOI) Act to obtain further insight into a public sector bid decision

The Freedom of Information Act (2000) is UK government legislation defining what information public sector organizations are obliged to provide on request from any member of the public. Only courts and tribunals and the security and intelligence services are not covered by the Act. For a full list of the authorities bound by the Act (pretty much every contracting authority), see **http://www.ico.gov.uk/for_the_public/official_information/authorities.aspx**. An authority can refuse to disclose the information requested only if there is an exemption in the Act that permits it to do so.

The Act can be a really useful learning tool for bidders in the public sector. For instance, you might wish to ascertain how competitive a particular process was (perhaps asking for information on the number of companies expressing interest, submitting PQQs and eventually being invited to tender). You may decide to request further information on the overall evaluation scores for a particular procurement process that you participated in (so that you can see others' scores, not just your own). You might even request copies of other bidders' documents.

It's purely up to you what you request, although you should bear in mind a few important considerations:

- You will not be able to request to see commercial information from any bid – this is covered by section 43 of the Act, which applies to trade secrets and to information that could otherwise prejudice a company's commercial interests. There's no point in requesting information about other bidders' prices, because these will not be released to you.

- Your request itself is in the public domain – unless you use an agency, your request might be visible to others, including those whose bidding information you are requesting. (If you're requesting a copy of a bid, for instance, it's likely that the authority will notify the bidder that a request has been made, and it may reveal the name of the requester, although not their personal information.) There's a way around this, if you'd prefer your name not to be associated with the request. Since anyone can make an FOI request, you could always ask a colleague, friend or family member to make the request on your behalf.

- You might have to pay – if the authority deems that the request will take more than a certain amount of time and therefore cost (*circa* 3.5 days or £600 for a government department, or 2.5 days or £450 for other authorities), it could charge you for access to the information. In any case, it is entitled to charge for copying and postage, although it doesn't always do this. Otherwise your request is free of charge.

- You won't necessarily get the information you request – the authority will decide whether, on balance, the release of the information is in the public interest or not. Most importantly, it will decide whether your request would prejudice national security or damage another company's commercial interests. If so, it will not release the information to you.

How to make your request
You can make a request directly:

- Find out the contact details of the freedom of information officer at the authority by contacting its switchboard.

- Create your request in writing (by either letter or e-mail), addressing your request to the relevant contact. You must provide your real name and an address to which the officer should reply. Your request must be dated. Although you don't have to, it's a good idea to include a phone number as well, in case the authority wants to speak to you about the request.

- Make it clear that you're making a freedom of information request. Be specific about what information or documents you're requesting. Use the tender reference (if one exists), and advise on the format in which you'd prefer to receive the information. Normally, this would be via e-mail or a hard copy, but you can request to see documents in person. Remember, there's no need to justify your request or to give a reason for making it.

You can use an agency. If you'd like someone else to do the legwork for you (not that there is a huge amount in the type of request we're talking about here), or if you don't want the request directly linked to you, there are a number of agencies via which you could channel your request. Some agencies will offer a service whereby they make the request on your behalf, and your identity is not therefore apparent to the authority or therefore to the other bidder(s) whose documents you've asked to see. You will have to pay for this service.

There are also free, online resources (such as **www.whatdotheyknow.com**) via which you can submit your request and track its progress. The name of the requester is clearly visible in these circumstances – not only to the authority but also to anyone visiting the site. In addition, the response from the authority to your request (including the documents or information requested) is also then made publicly available via the site.

What happens after the request is made?
Initially, you are likely to receive an acknowledgement from the FOI officer; this will be a standard response, noting the date and nature of your request.

The authority should then respond to you within 20 working days (there are some extensions allowed, but as a general rule this is the time limit set by the Act). Once this time has elapsed, the authority should either provide the information that you requested or tell you why it will not or cannot do so.

If you've requested copies of bids, don't be surprised if there are certain pages that are missing or passages blacked out. This is known as 'redacted' information. Commercially sensitive information (prices or trade secrets, for example) will be redacted, unsurprisingly. Also, personal information included in a bid (CVs or biographies of key personnel, for instance) might well be missing or blacked out.

Are FOI requests worth it?

In my time, I've made a fair number of FOI requests to various authorities – with mixed success! In many instances, the documents requested have arrived within a few days of the request being made. However, the process hasn't been so smooth in other cases. Where requests to see bids and evaluation have been refused, it's always been because of commercial sensitivity – I appeal these whenever it's prudent and timely to do so. But, since the appeals process is open-ended (there are no specified time limits for authorities to act upon them), this can be a draining and time-consuming activity.

On balance, I would say that making FOI requests is definitely worth the effort, but I'd recommend that you proceed with caution – remembering that bidders will be made aware of requests to see their documents, and the name of the requester. You'll have to decide the implications of this, according to your own circumstances.

Challenging an FOI decision

Of course, there are no guarantees at all that the information you have requested will actually be released. If the authority decides to refuse your request, it must tell you why, giving details of the relevant exemption that applies to your request. If the authority claims the public interest exemption, it must give you an explanation as to why it believes it is in the public interest not to disclose the requested information.

It's important to realize that, if your request is refused, you have a right to appeal (indeed, the authority should clearly state this fact and tell you about the process of lodging an appeal). Having challenged the authority's decision directly, you might eventually be led to the Information Commissioner's Office. Those engaged in ensuring that the freedom of information process works as intended would encourage you to appeal whenever you are not satisfied – they say that this is the only way to extend and increase the effectiveness of the legislation.

Protecting your own bids under the FOI Act

If you can use the Freedom of Information Act to look at others' bids, remember that so too can it be used for access to yours. There's nothing you can do to stop this, of course, but you can take steps to protect sensitive commercial and personal data that will undoubtedly be included in your bid documents.

In some public sector tender documents, the authority will include a schedule or appendix document in which it will invite you to list those aspects of your bid that contain information you would seek to protect under the Act. Other tenders make no reference to this, and so you will need to add your own statement or table of items you would seek to protect in your final bid submission. Either way, your request must detail:

- The information you are seeking to protect.

- The precise location of the information in your bid documents (make sure you identify each occurrence – so if you've included a commercial headline in your executive summary, for instance, don't forget to identify it as part of your request).

- The reason for including the information in your request. Ideally, you should mention the specific section of the Act. For instance, section 43(1) deals with trade secrets and section 43(2) deals with the commercial interest of the bidder and the authority.

- The proposed duration of the exemption period.

If the authority receives an FOI request for all or part of your bid, it may come back to you to confirm this fact and to notify you of the information it intends to disclose to the requester. As with all legal matters, you may wish to seek legal advice prior to submitting your bid, to ensure that your exemption request is as comprehensive as it can be.

Creating a knowledge base for future bids

In submitting any bid, you'll be creating material that describes your organization: what you do and how you do it. You'll be writing case studies that demonstrate your expertise, and you'll be recording successes and documenting policies. In short, you'll be creating a library of information that can be used again for future bids. If you think that you will be entering more bid competitions again in the near future, it's worth considering setting up a knowledge base in which to store the information you've gathered so far.

Depending on the amount of information you need to store, and the number of people who might need to contribute to or access it, you will need to arrive at an appropriate system for your knowledge base. A simple suite of folders on a shared network drive can be a very effective starting point. A 'wiki' system based on Microsoft's Sharepoint can also work well. There are many pieces of software available to support knowledge management, and you'll need to settle on the tool that is most appropriate to you and your contributors. It needs to be accessible but secure, easy to use and to update. However, the content is always the most important element of any knowledge base.

In overview, these are the steps you'll need to follow to create a simple but effective knowledge base:

1 Give one person the responsibility for managing the overall knowledge base project – a 'knowledge manager' if you like. Ideally, this person will have good administrative skills and will be able to write well. Almost as importantly, knowledge managers will need to be able to work well with contributors, persuading them to keep information relevant, up to date and fresh. Get your knowledge manager to draw up an action plan, working with contributors to collect up content for the knowledge base over a realistic time period.

2 Make a list of all the content that you are likely to need for future bids; place a higher priority on those topics that you think you'll be asked for regularly. Start with high-level headings (corporate profile, environmental management, financial reporting, HR, quality management, training, biographies and photos of key personnel, etc); then create sub-headings to make each subject more manageable.

3 The knowledge manager then needs to allocate a 'subject-matter expert' to each topic: the person within your organization who knows most about it. The knowledge manager should brief the subject-matter expert on the content that needs to be created. Contributors will need to be guided, receiving instructions such as how many words their piece should be, how detailed, what images, graphs or other diagrams they'll need to include, etc. If the subject-matter expert struggles with writing, try the 'interview and write up' approach, using those with a talent for writing from within your team or even an external copywriter.

4 Decide on a repository for the content that you're going to collect. Make sure that it's secure, user-friendly, and readily accessible to all potential contributors. If your team is spread across multiple locations, this will need additional consideration.

5 Ensure that your knowledge manager keeps up to date with new developments within your organization, adding new topics to the list as appropriate, and commissioning them from subject-matter experts in a timely manner. Outside of live bid processes, existing content should be reviewed regularly to ensure it's up to date and relevant. Recent bids should be reviewed (even those that you do not pursue), so that changing market demands are also reflected in the content of your knowledge base.

6 After each new bid submission, ensure that the knowledge manager takes any new or updated content and posts it to the relevant place in the knowledge base for future use.

Once you have a knowledge base, it will completely transform your approach to bidding. Each bid will become much quicker to complete, and the time allocated to populating standard questions will reduce dramatically. This will leave you with more thinking space for the tailored elements of your bid: the executive summary, the operational solution and the pricing proposal. It might feel like a lot of effort to start with, but if you're serious about bidding it will become one of your most valuable resources.

Measuring your bid performance over time

As you gain experience in bidding, you will hopefully commit increasing amounts of time and resource to associated processes. In this case, it will become important to know that you and your wider bid team are performing well and operating effectively.

Win rate

There is much debate amongst bid managers about which are the best key performance indicators (KPIs) for a bid function. Most will agree that 'win rate' is the headline KPI, and we introduced this idea at the beginning of the chapter. But when it comes to the way to calculate that rate – or indeed what the benchmark for a high-performing bid team should be – there is much debate. And, of course, there are a great many factors that can affect bid outcomes and therefore an organization's win rate.

The simplest way to calculate a win rate is:

$$\frac{\text{Number of bids won}}{\text{Number of bids submitted}}$$

But in a busy bid team there will always be some bids against which a decision has not yet been received, so these should be taken into account too. Your win rate calculation could then be:

$$\frac{\text{Number of bids won}}{\text{(Number of bids submitted – number of bids awaiting decision)}}$$

And then there might be bids withdrawn by the buyer; these shouldn't drag down your win rate, should they? So perhaps the calculation should exclude these too, in which case it should be:

$$\frac{\text{Number of bids won}}{\text{(Number of bids submitted – number of bids awaiting decision – number of bids withdrawn)}}$$

I've even seen interim bid managers or bid consultants, who have no influence on pricing strategies, use the following win rate calculation (which unsurprisingly elevates their win rate hugely!):

$$\frac{\text{Number of bids won}}{\text{(Number of bids submitted – number of bids awaiting decision – number of bids withdrawn – number of bids lost on price)}}$$

Since there's no absolute agreement of the definition of win rate amongst bid managers, then, it's difficult to compare like for like. I've heard some bid managers claim anything up to a 95 per cent win rate, but those managers might be operating in an environment in which an extremely stringent attitude to bid qualification is taken. Unless the bid decision is pretty much certain to go in their favour, they do not proceed. Or they might be an interim bid manager or a consultant, and opt to exclude bids won on price. Not surprisingly, then, their win rate would appear to be very high.

On the other hand, bid managers in emerging markets, where competition is not mature and suppliers operate on a more level playing field, might take a more open view of the bid decision, looking to learn and develop their offering with the market. They might enjoy a much lower win rate (of perhaps between 25 and 30 per cent) therefore.

In reality, it doesn't matter which calculation you use to measure your performance, but it is vital that you are consistent. Only in this way can you truly determine whether your performance is improving over time. For the record, I favour the third option of the four shown above. Using this calculation, I would expect a high-performing bid team to be achieving a win rate of over 50 per cent.

Other bid team KPIs

Win rate shows the percentage of bids you win, but doesn't tell you anything about the quality of those bids, nor how effective your resource management processes are. You could be artificially inflating your win rate with a high volume of low-value bids, for instance, never winning the high-value contracts that you'd really want. Or you could be spending a disproportionate amount of time on creating your bids.

Below, we will discuss two of the other most commonly used bid team KPIs that will help to balance the picture.

Effectiveness rate

Your effectiveness rate considers the value of the contracts won versus those submitted, as follows:

$$\frac{\text{Value of bids won}}{\text{Value of bids submitted}}$$

Again, as with win rate, you could exclude pending and withdrawn bids from this calculation, if preferred. (Whatever you do for your win rate, you must also do for your effectiveness rate, of course.) If your effectiveness rate is greater than your win rate, you are winning more of the larger opportunities, and your team is performing well.

Income versus opportunity cost

Of course, the effectiveness rate doesn't consider how much time and effort goes into each bid. So you may be competing in – and winning – a high number of small bids, but your efficient team whips through them very quickly, and they do not 'cost' a great deal. It's also useful to know what each pound sterling of business won has cost your organization in the first instance.

To do this, you'll first need to arrive at a cost per hour for bid activities, bearing in mind that some contributors may attract a higher or lower cost individually. You will then need to begin to record the number of hours spent on each bid by these contributors. Overall, this will build to a total opportunity cost. To arrive at a ratio that measures cost versus the income that this activity has generated, the calculation is simply:

$$\frac{\text{Value of bids won}}{\text{Cumulative opportunity cost of bids entered}}$$

This measure is best viewed alongside the other two headline KPIs (win rate and effectiveness rate) to ensure that effort is being expended in the right place. Clearly, over time, you are looking for your income versus cost metric to be continually increasing.

SUMMARY

Celebrate winning bids but don't get too despondent about losses – think of them as learning experiences and use them to improve.

Always ask for feedback from the buyer, whether you've won or lost. Similarly, always ask your internal team for insights into their experiences of the bidding process – what went well or not so well? Consider using freedom of information requests as part of your competitor insight and lessons learnt process. Whatever feedback you manage to gather, use it to learn and adapt so that you improve every time you submit a bid.

Use past bids as the building blocks of a knowledge base and then create new content ready for future bids. The resulting resource will make future bidding activity much more efficient – and effective.

As you continue on your bidding journey, analyse your performance over time, using a consistent set of metrics that ensure you are working to optimum levels.

A view from the other side
The buyer's perspective

THIS CHAPTER COVERS:

- A (very) brief history of tendering procurement

- The process of procurement – how it happens today

- What buyers would like to say to bidders

- The feedback I give to buyers

It's easy, as a bidder, to get paranoid about buyers – to feel that they're 'out to get you', that they exist just to make your life miserable! Put any group of bid managers in a room together and ask them what their pet hates about bidding are and they will invariably focus their attention outwards – to the principal person on the other side of the fence: the buyer.

Of course, this is wholly unreasonable (and most bid managers would accept this, if pushed), but it's an understandable viewpoint. So, in the interest of fairness and balance (and, of course, to help you to get better at bidding), it's time to think what life is really like for the buyer.

I try to meet buyers whenever possible, and to quiz them about what it's like to be the one in charge of the process. As a result I've met a lot of procurement people, from both the private and the public sector. And whenever

I've had the opportunity (outside of a live tendering process, of course) I've asked them about their experiences.

This chapter is a collection of the insight and knowledge that I've gleaned from these conversations. There are some themes that are almost universal, and of course I'll explain these, but there have also been some surprising admissions 'off the record', and I think these are just as valuable (naming no names, of course).

A (very) brief history of tendering procurement

If bid management is an emerging discipline, this is most definitely in response to the changing face of procurement, especially via tendering, over the last 30 years. In this time, developments in the way that public services are commissioned have been a forceful driver of procurement process change.

Throughout the 1980s the Conservative government introduced compulsory competitive tendering (CCT) in an effort to drive efficiency and competition in local government. With the outcome being a system heavily skewed towards price (quality seemingly less of a concern), the largely discredited notion of CCT had been replaced by the harder-to-define concept of best value by the 2000s.

In tandem with this, the European Commission adopted a set of public procurement directives in 2004, which were implemented into UK law in 2006 as the Public Contracts Regulations 2006 (in England, Wales and Northern Ireland) and the Public Contracts (Scotland) Regulations 2012 (in Scotland).

Add in the influence of the internet on tendering processes, and those tasked with putting contracts out to tender have operated in a very dynamic, ever-changing environment in recent times.

However, buyers will themselves admit that reaction on the procurement side has been inconsistent. So, whilst some pioneers have been busy designing, adopting and refining good practice at the earliest opportunity, others have lagged behind and are decidedly 'old school'.

It's my belief that, as a direct result of the EU's actions, the public sector has been leading the way in procurement best practice, and that the private sector, seeing the benefits, has followed swiftly along.

The process of procurement – how it happens today

Let's start, then, by taking a look at what the average buyer looks like.

The procurement professional

And here's our first challenge. There's no such thing as an 'average' buyer. For a start, only some of them will actually hold professional procurement qualifications, such as a graduate diploma from the Chartered Institute of Purchasing and Supply (CIPS), and will be active members of the Institute. There's no mandatory requirement for this qualification, or any equivalent, in either the public or the private sector (although, of course, employers may demand it as evidence of competence).

So buyers may or may not be experienced in running procurement processes.They might only procure a small number of contracts each year – or they might be managing multiple, large-scale, complex processes concurrently (or anything in between).

To further complicate matters, the process that they are managing might be bound by the EU regulations if they are operating in the public sector, but only if it's above-threshold – so then again it might not (go back to Chapter 2 for a reminder about above- and below-threshold levels). And if they are operating within the private sector they might have a defined procurement process to follow, with clear guidelines about supplier engagement – but then again they might not.

The point I'm trying to make is this: regardless of who is putting an opportunity out to tender, don't be fooled into thinking that buyers will run a 'perfect' tender process. They might, of course (but I truly haven't seen too many of those). Over time, you will find that the quality of tenders can be just as variable as the quality of bids!

Perhaps, then, it would be more useful to try to identify what makes a good buyer. Good buyers will:

- respect suppliers, recognizing what it might take to complete the tender that they are publishing;
- keep processes as simple as possible;
- give sufficient time for completing a bid, respecting bidders' holidays and other obvious time-related pinch-points;
- create the best conditions for the best possible deal;

- try to level the playing field (in the recognition that good bidders will do everything they can to un-level it!).

How buyers' performance is measured

All buyers will have their own key performance indicators: the aspects of their work that show whether or not they are being effective and to what degree. These will most likely include:

- management of their slice of their organization's procurement budget;
- the price they are able to secure for each contract – and how long that price is held;
- contract terms negotiation, and the balance of risk within the final agreement;
- stability of supply (ie whether or not a supplier will be able to meet its obligations throughout the contract term);
- ongoing quality of supplier performance;
- ease of contract management for those within their organization who have day-to-day contact with suppliers;
- signing of contracts in a timely fashion.

All buyers will have targets relating to some or all of these factors, so you should expect that these measures will dictate their behaviour during any process. This insight definitely helps to explain why they do things the way they do!

The procurement process – a simple overview

Now we've got a better idea of what good buyers look like, and what drives their behaviour, let's have a think about the steps they have to take before they can publish tender documents. (It must be noted that I'm summarizing and simplifying all of the steps of the procurement process in my descriptions below. This stuff is the content of another book!)

Deciding the type of competition to use

In the public sector, the regulations will offer some absolute rules about which procedure can and can't be used (see Chapter 2 for more information about the different types of procedure available to buyers). But there still exists some element of choice: whether to use an open or a restricted procedure, for instance. Recently, public sector buyers have been admitting that the government's push for more procedures to be run as 'open' rather than 'restricted' is not altogether welcome. Opening your tender to all-comers can create a huge burden for both buyers and bidders, they argue. It's better for all concerned to have a pre-qualification phase, as offered within the restricted process. (For the record, I totally agree.)

In the private sector, buyers might well wish to open up the opportunity to the widest possible marketplace, and could decide to run a shortlisting process, via a request for information (RFI), before moving to the invitation to tender (ITT) or request for proposal (RFP) stage.

If there is to be a pre-qualification or shortlisting phase, buyers must set about creating the set of information they require to identify the most credible and capable suppliers.

They then need to advertise the opportunity in the appropriate place, and start to engage with interested bidders.

Specifying a tender

Buyers will almost all agree that specifying a tender is the greatest challenge they face. Just as a bid manager will struggle to get the attention of subject-matter experts when responding to a tender, so will buyers similarly struggle with their internal stakeholders when creating it. Even once they are able to convince stakeholders to stop procrastinating and finally sit down and begin the process of specifying requirements, there can often be quite vociferous disagreement about how best to define the specification. Buyers have to navigate through these conflicting requirements, forced to arrive at a compromise all too often. They also have to separate out 'needs' from 'wants' to ensure that the final requirement doesn't end up over-specified and therefore unaffordable.

Alongside the specification element, buyers must choose the information they will need for their own purposes. They must ensure that they are identifying those suppliers who will ensure that buyers' own KPIs would be met in the event of a contract award. They must also determine the evaluation criteria, ensuring that they will result in the 'best value' outcome at the end of the process.

They will also need to determine the terms and conditions under which the contract will be managed, once awarded. This documentation will define exactly how buyers envisage the contract will be managed by both parties during the contract term. The proposed agreement might include risk and reward options, service penalties and credits, early completion bonuses, gainshare agreements and the like. When buyers draft this part of the document, they do so in the hope that it will be accepted by suppliers without amendment. They certainly do so with the intention of protecting their organization's interests, pushing as many risks to the supplier as possible. Once the procurement phase is over, this legal document will need to be signed by both parties.

Once drafted, all parts of the proposed tender must go back to stakeholders for approval. This can be a painful and lengthy process for buyers, with the documents often passing through multiple stages and enduring many changes until they are finally deemed ready to issue. And then the next round of fun starts.

During the bidding process

It's only when the documents hit the desks of potential bidders that buyers start to find out how the market is reacting to them. These can be tense times for buyers. If there's absolute silence from those who've received the documents, buyers might assume one of two scenarios: 1) No one's interested in bidding (disaster). 2) The instructions and specification are so good that no one needs any additional information from the buyer (utopia). (Actually, there is another possible explanation – that those tasked with bidding are up to their eyeballs in other tasks, and haven't quite got round to reading the document yet!)

The problem for buyers is, initially anyway, that they have no idea which scenario applies in their case. (That's why some buyers request that bidders confirm their intention to bid shortly after the issue of the tender documents. This can never be legally binding, and you can always withdraw your intention. The buyers simply want some comfort around numbers of likely bidders.)

If they do start to receive questions from the market, buyers then have to decide what action to take. Some questions will require buyers to go back to their internal stakeholders, who might be unwilling or even unable to provide further information. Other questions will be answerable by the buyers themselves: questions about the procurement process itself or clarification about submission instructions.

Sometimes, the questions raised will materially affect the specification. This is one of a buyer's worst nightmares, since it could mean that the deadline needs to be extended or – even worse – the whole process scrapped and restarted. Buyers really don't like this scenario. I mean *really* don't like it.

Evaluation

Assuming the bidding phase has passed off smoothly, completed bids will arrive and the day will come when buyers can start to oversee the evaluation process. Thus starts a new set of headaches.

The buyers will call an evaluation meeting as soon as possible after the deadline, to which all those who will be involved in evaluating bids will be invited (assuming the buyers are not simply scoring it themselves). At this session the buyers will coach evaluators on the scoring system, reminding them that they can allocate a score only to information provided in the bid itself. (Actually, whilst this is most definitely the case in the public sector, private sector evaluations are a little more *relaxed*, let's say.)

Once everyone has been briefed, buyers will send off the evaluators to do their thing. This is the most time-consuming aspect of the process and one that needs to be actively managed by buyers, to ensure progress. Buyers need to be absolutely certain that evaluation is fair and carried out as specified. Good buyers will audit and check all completed evaluations themselves to satisfy themselves that this is the case.

At this stage, of course, the bidders' prices are also evaluated. The way that the price is evaluated will be specific to that particular bid. (See Chapter 7 for further information on pricing evaluation techniques.) This is where a badly specified tender document starts to affect the effectiveness of the evaluation. In such cases, bidders will have interpreted the specification differently, and will have made different assumptions about what to include in their proposal. As a result, buyers are faced with the realization that they can't make like-for-like comparisons on price. They might then have no choice but to go back to bidders and ask for further clarification on how prices have been arrived at. This is not good, and buyers will want to avoid this scenario at all costs (if you'll excuse the pun).

If an e-auction is to be conducted, it is at this stage that buyers will issue notice and instructions about participation. Only those who are deemed to have successfully passed the technical evaluation (ie whose proposal fully meets the given specification) will be invited to 'attend' the e-auction. Others will be notified that they have been unsuccessful at this stage. (See Chapter 7 for further information about e-auctions.)

Finally, once all evaluations are complete, buyers will make a recommendation to award. To whom this recommendation is made and how the recommendation is ratified will be different within every organization. But this is the point at which buyers need to justify their decision to the powers that be and show the evidence for their recommendation. (And therefore the point at which your executive summary really comes into its own...)

Assuming an acceptance of the recommendation, buyers will then inform the winning bidder(s) – the nice part of their job, I suppose – and then notify all those who were not successful (the not-so-nice part).

If required, a standstill period will then ensue (in above-threshold competitions in the public sector), during which buyers will be sincerely hoping that no legal challenge is mounted by any of the unsuccessful parties.

In the private sector (and sometimes in the public sector) a period of due diligence will now take place – along with final contract negotiations. Private sector buyers might well take the opportunity to carry on the commercial negotiations at this time, too (just because they can, I reckon).

Managing feedback

With the contract award made, there comes the responsibility of public sector buyers (above-threshold at least) to provide feedback to unsuccessful bidders. Good buyers will take the long-term view on this and see it as a way of informing the market for next time, in the hope of getting a more competitive set of bids.

Private sector buyers will almost always ignore or stall over requests for feedback, or just tell you that you lost on price (not necessarily true, but the simplest way to justify their decision). I suppose this is understandable. By the time they've awarded the contract, this project has moved onto another phase and they don't want to waste any more time on it. In fairness, occasionally private sector buyers will engage with feedback requests.

What buyers would like to say to bidders

When I meet buyers, and ask them about their reaction to the bids they receive, they almost always start by telling me what they don't like. So let's explore these first.

Top 10 of buyers' dislikes

1 Waffle, boasting and flattery.
2 Missing information or incomplete responses.
3 Hidden or missing prices.
4 Hard-to-find information and multiple cross-references. (Evaluators often review only part of the submission. If one part of the bid cross-references to another part that the evaluator doesn't have sight of, this makes life difficult for all concerned.)

5 Unsubstantiated claims (ie descriptions of what will be achieved without any evidence of previous experience or case studies delivering similar results).

6 Jargon.

7 Bidders who make no attempt to clarify questions or information they don't understand and who therefore make incorrect assumptions.

8 Bidders who ask for information already supplied in the tender documents.

9 Requests for deadline extensions (buyers have a special contempt for bidders who don't leave enough time for production or submission and then plead for special dispensation or a deadline extension).

10 Non-compliant bids (bidders who effectively tell the buyer they have asked the wrong question, and present an alternative solution that doesn't meet the specification and that is therefore impossible to evaluate. Buyers do sometimes accept such proposals – known as variant bids – but only where a compliant bid is offered as well).

Top 10 of buyers' likes

1 Logical, well-constructed documents.

2 Evidence of capacity, capability and experience.

3 Compliant solutions that fully meet the specification.

4 Quantifiable value in the compliant solution.

5 Added value – this makes buyers look as though they've negotiated well, and it makes them feel useful and valuable in the process. (Examples buyers give of added value include: free training or consultancy; commercial innovations around fixed-cost treatments, such as deferment or spread of payment; extended payment terms, and also gainshare, but only if the mechanism is relatively simple, easy to evidence and evaluate, and clearly potentially valuable to the buying organization.)

6 'Owned' solutions (in which the bidder has indicated clear points of contact and demonstrates a focus on and commitment to contract and relationship management).

7 Innovation and fresh thinking in the proposed solution.

8 Respect for the process.

9 Clearly labelled submissions.

10 Evidence of the bidder's appetite for the work.

What buyers say to justify the things they do

I think buyers realize that bidders can be somewhat frustrated by the process, and often want to try to explain the reasons behind some of their actions. For instance, at various times I've been told:

- They don't like disqualifying bidders at the PQQ (or indeed any) stage; they do have sympathy for bidders who've made the effort, and who have fallen foul of a technicality, but they have a job to do.

- Short deadlines or badly timed tenders (for instance those timed to coincide with the Christmas/New Year break) aren't a deliberate ploy to test or even annoy bidders. Instead, buyers claim they are normally an indication of a slip-up, not a conspiracy! (I always check to see if they have their fingers crossed when they say this.)

- When time is short (and sometimes when it's not), buyers admit that they might well resort to using a template, or to issuing a 'cut and paste' tender (using documents from a previous process). I'm not sure bid managers are in a position to criticize this approach, to be honest! People in glass houses...

- Buyers use e-portals to make evaluation easier, and to enable them to compare like-for-like responses more quickly. This is especially true in competitions where high volumes of bids are expected, or where commodities are being bought.

- E-auctions are used to drive the price down, pure and simple (though buyers admit that this process works best for the purchase of commodities and less well when a service is being procured).

The buyers' plea to bidders

I'm passing on a message here; this is a compilation of the replies I've received over the years to the question 'If you could say one thing to bidders about how they should prepare their bid, what would it be?' These answers are straight from the buyer to you, so don't shoot the messenger, but do take note:

- Read the instructions and follow them to the letter!
- Never submit an incomplete document.
- Be concise, but ensure you provide enough detail for the evaluators to mark.
- Don't assume any prior knowledge on the part of the evaluator.
- Engage with buyers, but only outside of live competitions (buyers do undertake market stimulation and market scanning activities, but these happen before they specify a tender).
- Don't try to circumvent the rules by talking to stakeholders in the buying organization at any level during a live process without permission – this might be a disciplinary offence for the person approached, and could result in your disqualification from the process.
- Recognize disqualification criteria, and check with buyers if there's *any doubt* about the compliance of your response.
- Ask questions – show buyers your appetite for detail.
- Demonstrate your understanding of the requirements at every opportunity.
- Make your assumptions clear, especially in your pricing proposal.
- Quantify and substantiate your claims for the outcomes of your proposal.

Off the record

Conversations with buyers will inevitably end with a couple of off-the-record disclosures that bidders should be aware of. It would be churlish not to let you have these. Just don't ask me to quote my sources!

Private sector buyers do sometimes run competitions with no intention of making an award or changing the incumbent supplier

Yes, private sector buyers do admit to running competitions with the express purpose of benchmarking, that is, using tender exercises purely to get a better deal from an incumbent supplier, with whom they might be completely satisfied but from whom they need a reduced price, by showing them what other bidders are willing to offer and at what price. There is nothing what-soever to prevent a private sector buyer from doing this, and there is little risk to them.

Buyers can find the evaluation stage to be hard-going

Buyers privately admit that they find the evaluation stage is the worst for all concerned; reading bid submissions can be 'boring', and it's hard to keep the evaluators' interest, especially where there is a high volume of bids to mark. (Could this be the real reason that so many processes seem to lose their momentum after the submission deadline?!) The lesson from this is: make it as interesting and as easy as possible for evaluators, recognizing that they are only human!

Some buyers also admit that this is one of the reasons that more electronic, portal-based submissions are being used – they allow a machine to do some of the evaluation. But there are not too many buyers who would admit that this is a perfect system either.

Buyers welcome executive summaries

Whilst they only occasionally stipulate that bidders must include one, buyers do welcome a well-constructed executive summary at the beginning of a bid. If done properly, a short piece giving them the overall business case for the bid can be a very useful tool for the buyer as he or she goes on to evaluate the detailed submission.

It's a favourite question of mine to buyers: would you read an executive summary even if you didn't request it? I haven't met one buyer who has answered 'no' (yet!). I'm going to keep asking, but I don't really expect to get a different response any time soon.

Buyers rarely view suppliers as 'partners'

Being recognized by a customer as a 'partner' is, of course, an aspirational position for a supplier, since it implies longevity of relationship, trust and security. However, for a buyer, whose job it is to drive cost efficiency (amongst other things, of course), a relationship that is too 'cosy' might not facilitate the right outcomes. End-users of your service or product might not agree; for them, a close and collaborative working relationship with a supplier makes life much easier day to day. But a buyer has a different perspective, and might wish to maintain some tension in the relationship. Bear this in mind when writing your bid, and use the term 'partnership' with caution.

The rules can be bent, sometimes

Buyers know that, while it's their job to try to operate a fair process, bidders will be doing all they can to create an advantage for themselves, so they accept that bidders will sometimes try to bend the rules. Privately, most buyers admit that they will 'use their discretion' when running a process – more so in the private sector, of course. But even in the public sector, under regulated processes, buyers admit that they have some options for accommodating bidders as they try to gain that advantage – as long it doesn't go too far, perhaps resulting in a legal challenge later.

Buyers might accept additional, unrequested information (such as an executive summary, or a DVD summarizing the bidder's proposal). Such additional elements wouldn't be scored, of course, but they might well influence the evaluators' overall perception of the bid. Buyers might request additional clarification to allow a preferred bidder a second chance to provide information that will bring the bidder's score up to par. Similarly, they might allow bidders to send in a missing document at the PQQ stage, rather than disqualifying them. They might even allow in-process discussions about commercially confidential aspects of a bidder's solution.

However, the 'hampers at Christmas' approach (the giving of gifts or inducements) is almost universally condemned. In the current environment, even in the private sector, this sits pretty uncomfortably with buyers.

Buyers don't always read policies

I had always wondered whether buyers and evaluators actually read all those policy documents they demand from bidders. The most common answer is: not always. They'll check to make sure they look reasonable and seem to cover the right areas at the right level of detail, but they don't read every word, every time. (I'm not sure what you can do with this knowledge, really, but it helps to know, don't you think?)

What keeps buyers awake at night

After buyers have completed a procurement exercise and the contract is let, their involvement will continue in some form or other. In smaller organizations, they might be required to act as contract managers, monitoring and managing the performance of the supplier(s) to whom the award was made. Even if they pass this responsibility on to another person or department, they will still want to avoid the following scenarios, which might indicate that they did not manage the procurement process as well as they could have. The stuff of buyers' nightmares includes:

- Underperforming suppliers – if an organization has outsourced a contract, it does not want to have to devote unnecessary energy to bringing the supplier back on track. The contract might well impose financial penalties on poor performance, but the customer wants the job done, not the money back! In the public sector especially, such an outcome damages the commissioning organization's reputation just as much as it does the supplier.

- Suppliers that go bust – this might leave the customer with no means of supply, and they might need to go back out to tender to plug the gap. This could take too long, and leave the customer in an extremely vulnerable position in the interim.

- Unexpected invoices – if suppliers realize part-way through implementation or delivery that they hugely underestimated their costs or misunderstood the specification, they might look to the customer to accept these additional costs. If the buyer has no budget to accommodate the extra charge, there is a danger either that the job will not get completed or that quality will be compromised.

The feedback I give to buyers

Don't worry, when I talk to buyers, I don't just let them tell me about what life is like for them; I also try to let them know what it's like to be on our side of the fence. If I can, then, I tell them about the top things that we bid managers hate about procurement (in as diplomatic a way as possible, of course). Here's my list. Get in touch if you think it needs adding to!

Bidders' top 10 hates about procurement

1 Short deadlines.

2 Unclear, fiddly or overly complex instructions.

3 Heavy restrictions on communications and access to the buying team and end-users during a live process. It just makes devising the perfect solution so much harder.

4 Onerous contract terms that are ridiculously weighted towards the buying organization. (I know this will never change, but it's worth a mention, surely!)

5 The way that buyers focus so heavily on the bottom-line price, not recognizing (or perhaps not being able to evaluate) value or innovation.

6   The narrowness or vagueness of a specification, and the inability for bidders therefore to show that there might be a better way, without first having to go through the motions of showing a 'compliant' solution that they have no intention of delivering.

7   Buyers' perceived resistance to relationship building.

8   The difficulties of trying to sell a complex/specialist product or service to a buyer who doesn't have specialist knowledge.

9   Being forced to use an e-portal or to work within formatting restrictions that stifle creativity and kill nuance. Oh, and having to submit *any* written response (except prices) in an Excel spreadsheet!

10 The way that procurement teams don't always seem to stick to their own timetables for evaluation and decision making.

SUMMARY

There'll always be a huge divide between buyers and bidders, but understanding each other's perspectives goes a long way to bridging that gap. The better understanding you have of what life is like 'on the other side', the more likely your response will be in tune with the buyer's position. Try to develop communications with buyers, talking to them outside of formal processes, if at all possible. And always prepare your bids in the knowledge that a real person (or several people) will be tasked with reading and evaluating it.

Do whatever you can to keep in tune with advances in procurement processes, and with the strategies and performance measures of the organizations you are bidding to. This insight will pay rich dividends in the long term.

External funding bids and grant applications

Applying bid best practice in not-for-profit competitions

THIS CHAPTER COVERS:

- Types of grants/funding

- Finding funding sources

- Deciding which funds to bid for

- Managing the bidding or application process

Perhaps you've turned to this chapter because you work in a not-for-profit organization that needs to bid for external funds in order to maintain its work, or maybe you need some advice in obtaining a grant to develop your business. Whatever the reason, you'll be looking for external sources of funding, and you'll need to complete a written application or bid to explain to the funding body precisely why you need the funds and what will be done with them.

You'll probably recognize that the process for making funding bids or grant applications can be challenging and time-consuming. You'll also realize that you need to put forward the best possible bid or application to be sure of securing the funds you need.

This chapter will show you that the skills required when bidding for commercial contracts, as described throughout this book, are exactly the same skills that are required for external funding bids and grant applications. It will also give you specific and practical advice and guidance when bidding or applying for external funds, to help you improve your chances of success.

Let's start by looking at the main types of grants that are available.

Types of grants/funding

There are several types of grants available, and you need to be clear about what it is you're bidding for, before you begin your application. The main categories are:

- *project cost grants* – under which the funder will meet only the costs of running a specific project, and not your day-to-day overheads (also known as 'core' costs);

- *core and project cost grants* – under which the funder will meet both core and project cost streams;

- *capital grants* – under which the funder will help you to make one-off purchases that then become your organization's assets (things like buildings and vehicles);

- *revenue grants* – under which the funder will help you to meet key outgoings such as rent, rates and utilities.

Funding bodies will recognize that you might have multiple funding sources to support your organization, and will be aware that they are likely to be funding only a percentage of your costs, with the balance being funded from elsewhere. However, if you operate your finances in this way, you will need a robust cost-centre-based accounting process in place to manage this. Be prepared to demonstrate its efficacy during the bidding process.

Next, let's consider where you might begin your search for the right type of funding opportunities.

Finding funding sources

The process of finding suitable funding streams can be a daunting one. There are literally thousands of public bodies (and indeed private funders) that invite applications for funding and that make awards every year. Because of the sheer volume of funds and their individual award cycles, processes and entry criteria, it's not possible to list all the sources of funding here, so I'm just going to give you a starting point.

Broadly, funds and grants can be split into two discrete categories: community-related and business. My guess is that you'll be looking for funding in one or the other, but most of the main grant search registers cover both categories. To start your search, try some of the websites listed below.

Grantfinder (**www.grantfinder.co.uk**) is a central register for funding opportunities. This is a chargeable service, and prices vary according to your search requirements. From here you'll be able to set your search criteria so that you are seeing only the most relevant opportunities for your organization.

Grantfinder also offers a free service called Grantnet (**www.grantnet.com**), which you can access via 'host organizations' such as local authorities, councils for voluntary service and other support agencies. The idea is that you access the database, search for appropriate funding schemes in your area and then go back to the host organization for further support and advice in completing your application – although the seeking of assistance is not compulsory.

In a similar vein Grantsnet (**www.grantsnet.co.uk**) is a no-frills site offering a free search service for both community and business funds. Grantsonline (**www.grantsonline.org.uk**) offers a similar service, along with a weekly e-magazine called *Funding Insight*, which gives a round-up of new opportunities and those approaching their deadline. The **www.j4bcommunity.co.uk** website is also a good resource for community and voluntary sector projects. Its sister site **www.j4bgrants.co.uk** offers the same service for business grants.

Alternatively, the government's directgov website has excellent links for community-related projects. Go to **www.gov.uk** and search 'community and voluntary groups funding'. Here you'll find links and resources for a wide variety of funding sources, including local authority grants, central government funding and the National Lottery's Big Lottery Fund.

For government information on business grants, go to the Business Link website (**www.businesslink.gov.uk**) and search 'grants'.

Clearly, this is just the starting point for your search for suitable funds for your organization. The internet is an invaluable resource for searching for funding, and you'll find an almost overwhelming array of funding sources to research.

Deciding which funds to bid for

Does this mean that, because there seems to be a lot of opportunity out there, it's easy to obtain funds? Unfortunately not. Funds are finite, usually have significant conditions attached – and are allocated only after the completion of stringent, competitive processes that are usually many times oversubscribed. It's therefore really important that you don't end up wasting effort on unsuitable applications. In order to be sure that this doesn't happen, you'll need to consider carefully how strong your case actually is before committing precious time and resource to the bidding process.

In Chapter 4, we looked at the three 'big' questions that needed to be considered before going ahead and committing time and effort to any bidding process. Let's revisit them now. In the case of a funding bid or grant application, the first two are exactly the same; the third is only slightly amended to reflect the nature of the award:

1 Is it deliverable?

2 Is it winnable?

3 Is it financially viable?

As was discussed previously, unless the answer to each is a resounding 'yes', then you should not proceed. Look back at Chapter 4 and have a look at the types of things that needed to be considered in order to be able to make the right decision confidently.

Additional considerations in a funding scenario are as follows.

Is it deliverable?

Take a close look at what you would be required to deliver in return for the funding award. How much change would you need to implement in order to demonstrate that all requirements could be met? It's tempting to adapt your own strategy to meet the funder's requirements and, in the process, lose sight of your own core focus and philosophy. Make sure that your model is a good fit with the funder's and only proceed if it is.

Funders need reassurance that the organizations to which they make awards are well run, with firm governance processes in place and sound financial management in evidence. If you are seeking a relatively large award (in relation to your existing income), you will have to show how you will accommodate and manage the resulting additional workload, in terms both of corporate governance and of people or resource management.

Is it winnable?

Remember, this is a competition; others will also be submitting bids and applications, and not everyone will be successful. Be sure that you meet all the specified criteria and that you have a strong and compelling case to present. In the current climate, funding bodies are more concerned with the projected outcomes and less with how you are going to deliver them – although, as discussed above, you will need to demonstrate that you are credible and well managed. You will need to present expected results clearly and quantifiably as part of your bid.

Meeting the criteria

Funders will normally need you to meet several key criteria:

- *Location.* Are you in the right place to deliver the funder's objectives? Funders might have very specific geographic requirements that dictate that your project must be carried out within the fund's specified boundaries. If your project doesn't operate in the right area, you won't be eligible.
- *Project purpose.* What's your main focus? Is there a good fit with the work that you do and the funder's vision and objectives? Will the outcomes of your work or project match with the funder's requirements? Unless there's a demonstrable similarity of vision between you and the funder, you are unlikely to be awarded any funds.
- *Organization type and size.* You might need to have a particular legal status (as a charity or a fully constituted community group, for instance) for the funder to work with you. Alternatively, you might need to work in a specified industry or sector. Similarly, the funder might be looking to support projects of a very specific size or those at a particular stage in their development cycle. (Some funders will not make awards to projects that are already under way, for instance.) Be sure that you fit the required profile.

Of course, there are likely to be other criteria or conditions specific to the particular fund. If you're not sure what the criteria are, talk to the funding organization and check exactly what they're looking for. This will save time for them and for you in the long run, so you should not meet any resistance to this request. Unless you have a strong match against all of the key criteria, don't waste your efforts. Look for a closer match; when you find a funder with which you are demonstrably aligned you will have a much stronger chance of winning.

Demonstrating the case for funding for your project

The funding body will have their own vision for the impact that their funds will have, and you will need to demonstrate clearly that you will be able to help them to realize this vision. They will not be interested in the effect that the fund will have on the immediate recipient (ie your organization). Their interest is in the ultimate beneficiary: end-users, customers, communities or target groups.

When considering the 'winnable' question, there are two vital considerations that you will have to make and for which you will need to show evidence. These are outlined below.

Demonstration of need

Many funding bids fail because applicants have failed to convince the funder of the need for the work they wish to carry out. The starting point for every funding bid should be a thorough assessment of the problem or issues that your work seeks to solve. In demonstrating need, you will need to undertake research, using a variety of sources. You should seek credible, external sources of statistical data, for instance, to show that the need for your work is defined and recognized.

As importantly, you should consult with those who will benefit from the work you intend to carry out. Indeed, the majority of funders will demand evidence of consultation with the eventual beneficiaries of your work. The way that you conduct such consultations will, of course, depend on your work and on the beneficiaries themselves. There is no prescribed way of carrying out the consultation, although you will need to be able to present your findings in such a way as to show that your consultation was worthwhile and delivered meaningful insight into the need.

The types of issues you could incorporate into your consultation could include some or all of the following:

- What is the consultees' assessment of the need or problem?
- What would happen if the proposed work was not carried out?
- Who would directly benefit from the work you would do?
- What would be the short- and long-term benefits of tackling the need?
- Would there be any other, indirect beneficiaries of the work?
  If so, who, and how would they benefit?

Funders will be able to visualize the need for your work if you can introduce a more 'human' element into your presentation. This can be done through case study stories, for instance, which help to create a stronger all-round case. Funders very much favour proposals that demonstrate that beneficiaries will themselves be involved in the planning and delivery stages. If you can provide evidence of the engagement and involvement of real people in your project, you are much more likely to be successful.

Look for the widest possible benefits that your project will promote (for instance, how helping individuals in a particular area will benefit the whole community), to improve your chances further.

Outcomes

Once the need for your work has been identified and presented, you will then be required to present a set of demonstrable outcomes to show exactly how your work will solve or improve the problem that you have thus far described. In the current funding climate, your outcomes are a vital aspect of your proposal, and you will need to spend time deciding what they will be. They must be SMART, for a start (specific, measurable, achievable, realistic and time-bound). They must also show how the situation will improve, measuring this change against the existing position.

Is it financially viable?

When considering this question, you will need to cost up the delivery of your proposed project over the given timeframe, and determine whether the funds available will be sufficient to meet your outgoings in this instance. In many cases, you will be required to show your budget as part of the application, so that the funder can judge how sound your financial planning is. They need to eliminate as much risk as possible from the decision.

Of course, a single application is likely to be a part rather than all of your income, and you might need to demonstrate how this funding stream would sit in the bigger picture. Either way, it is imperative that you adopt sound budgetary disciplines when creating your financial plan. Be sure that you consider all the 'hidden' costs that your proposal might include: administration, facilities overheads, even reporting progress back to the funder. All will take time, effort and therefore, unless you have willing volunteers, money.

Once you have a clear picture of the costs involved, be sure to be realistic about how the total amount you require stacks up against the funds available. Look at the funding body's guidelines to determine this. They often wish to award to several projects, rather than one, so there's little point in bidding for the entire 'pot'. If there's any doubt, speak to the funding body to ascertain whether there are minimum or maximum bids that they will consider. You might then have to adapt your plan accordingly.

Matched funding

It's becoming increasingly common to stipulate a 'matched funding' require-ment, whereby the funder will contribute only a certain percentage of the required funds. The remainder has to come from other sources, and you will be required to confirm that this is the case. When researching for comple-mentary funds (ie multiple sources of funding that you will be able to use in a matched funding environment), be sure to look closely at the phasing of the awards. In most cases, funds will need to be available to you at the same time in order to satisfy the conditions for matched funding.

In-kind provision

Of course, there may be instances when, instead of monetary matched fund-ing, you receive 'in-kind' contributions that support your projects. Such ar-rangements might be in the form of volunteers, donated consultancy or the receipt of donated products or services. Whilst these arrangements may not have a financial basis, they will have an equivalent monetary value, which you will need to calculate and provide evidence of. Funding bodies will often accept the value of these in-kind contributions as matched funding.

Managing the bidding or application process

Once you have made the decision to proceed with the bid, the process itself will follow a very similar course to any other form of bid. Refer back to Chapters 5 and 6 for advice on navigating your way through the process and on creating a winning written submission. Then flick forward to the 'golden rules of bidding' in Chapter 14. Remember, when reading these chapters, that the funding body is your 'customer', and you should be doing everything you possibly can to prepare a customer-focused bid.

There are just a few extra tips and hints to bear in mind when you are applying for funding (rather than for a commercial contract). These are:

- *Plan your funding requirements well in advance.* Sometimes the decision-making process can seem to take for ever during funding applications. Of course, in other cases, the whole process is swift and painless, but these do seem to be the exception rather than the rule. You'll need to plan your future funding requirements well in advance and then commence the search for relevant sources in good time, taking into account the probable duration of the whole process.

Again, a dialogue with the funding body will help you to determine this in each case.

- *Don't start the project before you apply for the funding.* Most funding bodies need you to demonstrate that you couldn't proceed with a project without their support. If your project is already under way, this weakens this argument significantly.

- *Try to bid as early as possible in the funding cycle.* In the public sector, funding cycles are often designed to synchronize with the government's financial year, which starts on 1 April in the UK. Ideally, you should try to make your bid or application as soon after the 'pot' is opened, to increase your chances of success. Otherwise, you might find that all the funds have been allocated and you've missed out. Talk to the funding body and try to coordinate with their timetable.

- *Build relationships for the future.* Once you've been awarded funding, it should be much easier to apply for a renewal of that funding (if available, of course – some funders will make only one-off awards), assuming that you manage your relationship with the funding body well. Naturally, this will mean delivering on the outcomes that you promised in your original application. It will also mean reporting back on your performance and showing your successes. Remember to say 'thanks' once you've got the funds, and build your relationship from there. It's vital that you adhere to all reporting requirements during the course of the funding, so that the funder knows you are using the money as intended and are reaching key milestones and outcome targets. Invest in your own long-term future by treating the funding body as a valued customer and you won't go wrong.

- *Preparing a successful submission (or not preparing a losing one!).* It has to be said that there is an element of luck in applying for grants, and you won't always be lucky, I'm afraid. You may get your bid in just after the pot dries up, or another project, slightly more aligned to the values of the funder, might be more appealing than yours. However, there are some things that you can definitely control to at least avoid your bid being rejected on a technical issue. The most common mistakes made in preparing funding bids or grant applications are:

  - omitting to include required information;
  - failing to demonstrate a clear need for the project through research and evidence;

- not meeting one or more of the given funding criteria;
- focusing on how the project will be delivered, rather than the outcomes and successes it will achieve;
- failure to demonstrate good project and financial management principles, thus introducing an unacceptable level of risk in the evaluator's mind.

If you ensure that you have avoided these pitfalls, you will not have prepared a losing bid. And, if luck is on your side, you might even have prepared a winning one.

SUMMARY

When searching for funding opportunities, make sure that the funding body's requirements are complementary to your own strategy and that you are not proposing a (potentially non-core) activity just to obtain the funds. Make a sound judgement call – don't be dazzled simply by the prospect of the income.

Plan your funding requirements well in advance and maintain regular searches for suitable funds. Bear in mind the cycles and timeframes over which awards are made and bid in good time. Prepare your proposed budget for your bid very carefully, ensuring that all the right elements are included. Be prepared to show how this fits into your overall business plan.

Ensure your organization is in good shape and can meet all the funder's criteria before committing time and resources to a bid. If your model requires you to manage multi-funded projects, you'll need to be able to demonstrate exemplary financial governance to each funder.

When preparing your bid, be sure to have a really sound case for demonstrating the need for your work, and a clear picture of the difference that it will make, through a set of measurable and desirable outcomes. Bids that show that the target audience are fully engaged in the proposed work are also much more likely to succeed.

Increase your chances of success by preparing a bid that concentrates on outcomes that match the funder's high-level vision. If you're not successful, adopt a lessons learnt process to understand why not. If possible, build a relationship with your funder(s) with a view to the future.

Proposals
Using bid writing skills in proactive selling processes

THIS CHAPTER COVERS:

- What is a proposal?
- How to construct an effective proposal
- Presentation and delivery of your proposal
- Follow-up

What is a proposal?

Right at the start of this book, I introduced the concept of a proposal being a proactive sales document. Unlike a bid, which is produced in response to a tender or set of instructions from the buyer, a proposal is created by the seller, to address a perceived or acknowledged customer need. When you write a proposal, you are effectively creating a business case for meeting that need.

In some cases, the document will be expected: perhaps when a face-to-face meeting or telephone conversation has gone well and the buyer asks you for further information. In other cases, you will send it entirely speculatively, in the hope that it will command the attention of the recipient.

Proposal documents are therefore designed to create interest in a product or service solution, with the ultimate aim of securing an order. A good proposal must therefore be:

- Customer-focused – recognizing the customer's vision and challenges, and addressing a specific and relevant need (even if customers have not recognized the need themselves).

- Compelling – easy to understand, offering real and tangible benefits against the identified need.

- Succinct – no need for too much detail in a proposal. This is about 'concept' selling: persuading a buyer that an idea is worth pursuing to a greater level of detail.

- Self-contained – it should enable the reader to make a decision based on its contents, even if that decision is to invite you to provide more detailed information.

How to construct an effective proposal

Often, those who need to write proposals are a bit stuck as to where to start, so they start talking about themselves or at least their organization. But, just as a bid should be created to meet a customer's specific needs, so must a proposal.

Don't lose sight of the fact that a proposal needs to be a self-contained document; this might be the one and only time you get the buyer's attention. It needs to be well constructed, logical and not overly pushy. Try not to come across as boastful; show instead why you are rightfully proud of your achievements. Anticipate any potential objections the buyer might raise, and address them within your document. Demonstrate the value of your proposition, showing the return that the buyer can expect on an investment. In this way you'll be skilfully constructing a complete business case for the buyer, which should aid the buyer's decision-making process significantly.

With all this in mind, below is a list of things I recommend you put into your proposal to make it as effective as it can possibly be (many of the skills and techniques you have been learning about in this book are the same ones you will need when creating a really powerful proposal, as in my view writing a proposal is a very similar activity to writing an executive summary for a bid; you may find it useful, therefore, to revisit Chapter 6 in conjunction with this chapter to obtain a complete picture):

1 *Introduce the need.* As obvious as it sounds, start at the beginning, with an explanation of why you've written the proposal (and therefore why you expect the recipient to continue reading!). Tell the recipient about the need you've identified and give a statement of how your proposal will meet this need. Give a clear and quantifiable benefit statement that includes a projected outcome or set of high-level benefits.

2 *Introduce yourself as the supplier best placed to meet the need.* Next, you need to move the reader to the realization that only you can meet this need – after all, you don't want your proposal to end up generating an order for a competitor! Therefore you'll need to introduce your differentiator: the reason why the buyer should place the order with you and not look elsewhere to meet the need. Try to reflect your organization's personality and uniqueness, which are the things that will most likely be your differentiators anyway. But avoid looking as though you're bragging or overstating the case. This is a difficult balancing act, so consult with colleagues if you think you've gone too far one way or the other.

3 *Outline how you would meet the need.* At this stage, a very brief overview of your technical or operational solution will allow the reader to ascertain the practical way in which you would deliver the solution. As with any buying decision, the buyer will be looking for evidence of control, governance, risk mitigation and reliability. Of course, if you have a particularly innovative or novel way of delivering the solution, be sure to include it in this section.

4 *Provide evidence of your experience and capability.* As we discussed in detail in Chapter 8, the buyer needs to be reassured that you are appropriately experienced to deliver the outcomes you are promising. Make mention of at least two customers for whom you have delivered comparable solutions and outcomes. As always, quantify the benefits the customers enjoyed. Include brief testimonial quotes in call-out boxes. Offer references from the same customers. As with the rest of the document, though, keep it brief. You can always provide much more detail later, if required.

5 *Show your price, alongside your value proposition.* I know a lot of sales people prefer to create the need before giving a price and therefore do not include any indication of cost in an initial proposal. However, since the one question that you can absolutely guarantee that a buyer will ask is 'How much?', it doesn't make sense not to

give an indication of price in a proposal. Otherwise, in my experience, buyers will either be annoyed or will make their own judgement about the likely price and why it's not shown. They may well conclude that you believe it's too high and might put the buyer off, which is why you haven't included it. Not only should you show a price, then, but you should also demonstrate its value by giving an overview of your value proposition (revisit Chapter 7 for further detail on what this means).

6 *Show project timescales.* In this section, you'll need to give an indication of how long it will take to implement the solution and when the buyer can expect subsequently to start seeing a return on the investment. As previously, if you can make reference to relevant past experience, this will reassure the reader greatly.

7 *Summarize and outline the next steps.* Reiterate the main benefits that customers will enjoy should they make the decision to proceed with you. If you feel it is appropriate, include a short overview of your organization at this point of the document. In the closing paragraph, give a clear idea of what will happen next in the process – that you will follow up the written proposal with a telephone call or a personal visit.

8 *Use attachments or additional information carefully.* If you feel it appropriate, you might wish to include additional information with your proposal, such as product samples, a company brochure, or standard terms and conditions. Of course, this is up to you, if you feel it will help the recipient to make the decision to proceed to the next stage of discussions. However, beware of diluting the effect of the proposal document itself by submitting other documents that are less tailored and that might detract from your core proposal.

9 *Contact details.* You should always include your contact details prominently in the document. In fact, as with an executive summary within a bid, you should always put your name, role and date at the end of your proposal to make it clear that you are the primary contact should the buyer wish to follow it up.

Presentation and delivery of your proposal

Of course, each proposal will be created from different circumstances, and you will need to decide how best to present your document and deliver it to the buyer. Clearly, this is an important sales tool and should be treated as such. Go for a non-gimmicky, professional presentation, making sure that there are no typos or other errors that will undermine your credibility.

If you've decided to present it in hard copy, consider delivering the document by hand to show its importance. If this is not possible, at least send it by recorded delivery to be certain it arrives on the buyer's desk with a little more authority than the day's other mail. Alternatively, if you're using e-mail to send your proposal, convert the file to a pdf to be sure it looks exactly as you intended when it is opened on the recipient's computer.

In all cases, the text of your covering letter/e-mail is just as important as the proposal itself, so give this as much thought as the main document. State the single most important benefit in the covering communication, to ensure that the buyer is sufficiently 'hooked' and wants to read on.

Follow-up

Once your proposal is safely delivered, don't leave it up to the reader to make the next move. It's your proposal and it's up to you to move it along to the next stage. Don't wait for the buyer to call you. Give the buyer an appropriate amount of time to read the document and then call to gain his or her feedback and, hopefully, to agree the next step in the buying process.

SUMMARY

Construct your proposal so that it is a complete business case for the buyer: a succinct and compelling document that spurs the recipient into action.

However, as well as presenting a strong case for action, make sure it promotes *your* organization as the supplier of choice. You don't want the buyer to take your idea and eventually award the contract to one of your competitors.

Write your proposal so that it is entirely customer-focused, concentrating on benefits and outcomes, not delivery methodology.

Present your price with confidence, alongside your value proposition. Don't be tempted not to show a price, hoping that the buyer will be sufficiently intrigued by your proposal to come and ask you how much it would cost.

Once you have submitted your proposal, don't wait for the buyer to call you. Be proactive and ask the buyer for permission to proceed to the next stage of the buying process.

The golden rules of bidding

14

Things I wish I'd known when I wrote my first bid

Below follows my list of golden rules that I always follow on any bid, regardless of size and complexity. I wish someone had given me this list all those years ago when I tackled my first bid. I'm giving it to you now so that you don't have to make all the mistakes that I made.

The list comprises, rather uncomfortably for the superstitious, 13 rules – but hopefully they'll bring you only good luck.

Happy bidding!

1 *Look for opportunity.* There are numerous ways of getting to hear about new opportunities, so keep your ears (and eyes!) open. Start a systematic campaign to target selected prospects, join your local chamber of commerce, sign up to the right public sector registers and talk to buyers. There are loads of opportunities out there, but you'll need to actively hunt them out.

2 *Don't bid for everything.* Be sure that the opportunity is winnable, deliverable and profitable (financially viable in the case of external funding bids) before committing to bid for it. Otherwise it could be a waste of time and effort. Don't be tempted to enter more and more bid competitions in an attempt to improve your chances of winning. Trust me, the throw-enough-mud-and-hope-something-sticks philosophy was never meant for the world of bids. Bid less; bid better; win more. Simple.

3 *See things from the buyer's perspective.* Buyers want to see how your proposition is going to meet their requirements and provide more benefits than anyone else's. They need to be able to justify selecting you over any other bidder, so give them the right information to help them to do so. Concentrate on what they want to buy, not what you've got to sell.

   With that in mind...

4 *Prepare your bid theme and executive summary first.* Be clear about what you're proposing; identify your differentiators. Set your bid theme (the overarching benefit of choosing you: things like experience, innovation, low-risk transition, cost efficiency, quality, end-user satisfaction – it'll be different each time, according to the customer's situation) and plan out your executive summary. You don't need to actually write it at the beginning of the process – but you should know what it's going to say.

5 *Look for showstoppers/important topics.* Make sure that you've got a fully compliant solution and that there isn't anything that you just can't deliver. Identify the parts of the bid that are the most important to the buyer (from the evaluation criteria given to you or from conversations you've had with the buyer) and tackle these first. As you progress with the bid, if there are still some big and seemingly insurmountable problems, refer back to golden rule number one. If you can't deliver it, should you still bid?

6 *Answer all the questions.* Don't be tempted to miss anything out – you'll lose vital marks! In a similar vein, make sure that you are certain that you have included everything the buyer needs in your submission. Sometimes a buyer will inadvertently ask for a policy document, say, in one part of the ITT but miss it off the response template. Read and reread the requirements to be sure you miss nothing. Often, when bids are scored, a very small margin will separate the first-placed bid and the runner-up. You can't afford to waste a single point.

7 *Answer the question the buyer is actually asking.* Look at the question and be certain that the answer you're planning to write actually gives the buyer what is needed. Try to read between the lines. Why is the buyer asking about this? What problem is the buyer trying to solve or what issues does the buyer want to avoid? Don't just cut and paste everything you have on the subject and hope the buyer can find something of interest buried in there. Tailor your answer to the question.

8   *Engage, influence and persuade.* Get to know your buyer; ask questions. Buyers want suppliers to provide the best possible solutions. Don't miss the opportunity to engage and show your appetite for the work. In the meantime, build relationships with other stakeholders and influencers within the organization. Ideally, you'll have done this work before the opportunity went to tender, but don't despair if this is a new relationship. It can still be done.

9   *Ascertain your price and know its value.* Since price is often the ultimate differentiator in a bid, you'd better make sure you get it right. Bear in mind the buyer's budget range, what it would take to provide a just-compliant solution and any added value that you can demonstrate. Don't try to hide your price at the back of your bid; include it in your executive summary (as at least a headline about your pricing strategy) alongside a summary of your value proposition.

10 *Follow the buyer's rules.* It's the buyer's process. Break the rules and buyers won't like it. (And you won't win.)

11 *Use case studies to reassure the buyer of your capability.* Back up claims and assurances of good practice with case studies and testimonies from past customers. Offer references even if they're not asked for. The buyer wants to avoid the risk that an untested supplier might pose. If you've got the experience, tell the buyer about it – this could be the differentiating factor between you and your competitors.

12 *Be organized.* Take some time at the start of the process to plan a timetable, and stick to it. Appoint a bid leader. Make sure everyone involved is clear about their contribution: what is expected and when. Plan in a little contingency. You can always use it for reviewing! Ensure you leave enough time for constructing, producing and delivering the final response document(s). Leave nothing to chance.

13 *Learn and improve.* Win or lose, conduct an internal lessons learnt review and ask the customer for feedback. Build a picture of your strengths and weaknesses relative to your competitors'. Build a simple knowledge base: a library of useful information for future bids. And never make the same mistake twice.

Based on a true story... the good, the bad and the ugly

15

Real-life examples from the world of bids

THIS CHAPTER COVERS:

- The good – the London 2012 Olympic bid
- The bad – techniques to avoid
- The ugly – how not to do it

The good – the London 2012 Olympic bid

When it comes to 'good' bids, there's one that stands so far above the rest that I knew I couldn't write this book without including it. Featuring a celebrity cast, plot twists aplenty and the definitive fairytale ending, the story of this bid is an inspiration to anyone who's ever started a competition with the odds stacked against them. It's a bid that has parallels with the smallest of bids, and it can teach us an awful lot about the art of winning. It is London's bid for the 2012 Olympic Games.

Because it's such an epic story, I can't possibly cover all the details of this inspirational bid here, and in fact I don't need to: Mike Lee, the bid's Director of Communications and Public Affairs, has done just that in his excellent and insightful account *The Race for the 2012 Olympics* (2006). I suggest you read that for the complete inside story.

Rather, I wanted to see if there were lessons to be learnt and inspiration to be gleaned from the process that resulted in the award being made to London – the underdog of the competition – in July 2005. I was intrigued to find out what it was like to have worked on such a long and complex project, and to find out whether the good practice that was clearly employed by the London bid team could be transferred into the smallest of bid teams working on their own 'Olympic' bid.

I approached David Magliano, who had been the bid's Director of Marketing from 2003 and who I knew had been the driving force behind the final presentation that sealed the win for London in 2005. His immediate reaction was that he believed a great deal could be learnt from his experiences. Even better, he was happy to share them with me.

What follows here, then, is David Magliano's inside view of the most competitive Olympic bid of all time, and how we all can learn and benefit from it.

The decision to bid

Clearly, the decision to bid for an Olympic Games is not one that is ever taken lightly. In London's case it took years of deliberation and lobbying before the decision to register the capital as a candidate city was finally taken early in 2003. Just submitting the bid was going to cost in the region of £30 million. And Paris, already established as the firm favourite, had been preparing since 2001, a full two years earlier. But the prize would be staggering and the opportunities for the regeneration of the city unparalleled. The balance of risk seemed acceptable. London would bid.

David Magliano joined after this decision had been taken, but had to make his own choice about committing to a project of this scale and complexity, in which there could be no guarantee of success.

He had previously worked with the then chair of the bid, Barbara Cassani, in the setting up of BA's budget airline, Go, and when she invited him to join the bid he had little hesitation in agreeing to join the team, even though he had no experience of 'big bids' before. He felt 'extreme familiarity' with the idea of creating a team from scratch with Barbara Cassani, and he felt confident that the bid would be run to the highest possible standards.

In David Magliano's case, it was the knowledge that a strong and effective leader would be chairing the bid that gave him the reassurance he needed to commit the next two years to the London bid.

Assembling the right team

When David Magliano joined the bid, he was perhaps only the third person on the payroll of what was essentially a start-up organization. Not only did the leadership team need to recruit for positions within the bid team itself, but they also needed to create all the support roles that would keep the team running: roles like IT, HR and accounts.

David Magliano recalls a period of uncertainty and ambiguity at the outset, as indeed he had anticipated, with this being a brand new company. This was familiar territory for him and Barbara Cassani in terms of creating a start-up, so decisions had to be made as to what resources would be needed, how the team would be structured and where time should be focused.

As a result, Magliano describes the first few months as 'chaotic', and he recalls a sense of having jumped in at the deep end. With the pressure of media scrutiny and the demand to see progress, I get the sense that, behind the doors of the bid's Canary Wharf offices, these were challenging and anxious times.

The team that eventually emerged from this planning phase comprised around 100 people, organized into three key areas:

1 The technical team: tasked with creating the bid document in response to the International Olympic Committee's RFP document and published instructions.

2 The marketing and communications team: tasked with managing the presentation of the bid, building public support and helping to present the technical documents to the IOC. This team would also be responsible for raising sponsorship for the bid itself.

3 The lobbying team: tasked with influencing the voting members of the IOC (those making the final decision) through a programme of activity that needed to be very carefully managed because of the very specific rules of engagement laid down by the IOC.

There was also a very clear need to work with all the other stakeholder groups that might themselves influence the IOC electorate and that therefore needed to be informed and persuaded about the London bid themselves. This role was taken on by the marketing and communications team in recognition of the fact that these other stakeholders (government, venue owners, sponsors, local residents' groups, athletes and many more – the team engaged with over 1,000 stakeholder groups in the course of the bid) had their own agendas and challenges to manage and could themselves be a very influential force either for or against in the eyes of the voting members.

So the team was well organized: a strong leadership team was in place and the various roles and responsibilities were well defined. Everyone was dedicated to the bid full time; no one was squeezing in a bid role alongside the day job (how your average bid manager would love this scenario!). However, as all the other bid teams were in the same position, Magliano doesn't feel that this resulted in any competitive advantage.

The stage was set to start creating the winning bid strategy.

Research and access to information

An Olympic bid is very much conducted in public, unlike the majority of bids that you and I will ever work on. This presents huge challenges to the bid team, but also means that they have access to information about not only historic bids but also the current bids of their competitors. This can give a fantastic insight into previous winning and losing strategies, and also the core messages that other candidate city bids are promoting.

David Magliano attributes 'enormous value' to this kind of information, and the London bid team spent a lot of time on this phase. At IOC headquarters in Lausanne is housed a library of all the previous Olympic bid documents, and this was a vital resource to the London bid team. Additionally, the team had access to key members of the teams from the previous British Olympic bids for Birmingham and Manchester. Intelligence on the other candidate cities' bid campaigns was compiled and used to ensure that true differentiators were identified and promoted. Magliano accepts that a good deal of 'smoke and mirrors' activity takes place between the bid teams over the course of an Olympic bid competition, and that information has to be separated from misinformation. But the awareness of your predecessors' mistakes and your competitors' proposal themes is indeed a powerful tool. The London team built their eventual proposition in the knowledge of what other cities had to offer, and were able to play up their own relative strengths in the context of others' weaknesses.

Creating the vision

I was fascinated to discover how the technical team and the marketing and communications teams worked together to construct a vision for the London

2012 Games and to write a technical bid to support that vision. In fact, my assumption that everyone would have a clear vision to follow from the outset turned out to be completely incorrect!

David Magliano explains that the creation of the London 2012 vision was 'iterative and messy'. He describes the fact that there was only a very fuzzy vision initially and how it was only after the technical bid started to develop that the marketing teams could look for unique elements that could be 'back-rationalized' into an overall vision. As these strategic ideas began to emerge, the two teams worked together to strengthen the proposed elements. The marketing team would look for ways in which the technical team could adapt the proposals to further strengthen the emerging vision, and the technical team would find solutions to allow the required benefits to be worked into the bid.

So, for instance, the idea of an athlete-centred Games, one in which the athlete's accommodation would be adjacent to the competition venues to minimize travelling times, was back-created. The technical team had a very limited set of options for designing the layout of the Games, since fixed geographical constraints meant that only certain areas of land were ever going to be available in Stratford, East London. David Magliano's team's research had identified that, in modern Olympic history, there had never before been a Games at which the Olympic Village had been part of the Olympic Park. A differentiator therefore began to emerge: London's bid would be designed for the convenience of the athletes, allowing them to perform better, not requiring them to waste time and energy travelling to and from their competition venue. From here a very persuasive message could be created and the benefits of this arrangement presented as one of the principal visionary elements of the bid.

Creating the technical bid

The written bid that was eventually submitted (after London's initial applicant questionnaire had seen it placed on the shortlist of five cities) ran to 600 pages in three volumes covering 17 themes, written in French and English. You can see these documents online if you're interested, by visiting **http://www.london2012.com/about-us/publications** and searching under 'Candidate file'. You'll find beautifully constructed documents, with no gimmicks (Magliano is dismissive of any such tricks in this environment), painting the vision for London's hosting of the Games, and covering the detail of all the IOC's required elements from accommodation to technology and absolutely everything else in between.

Apart from the sheer scale of the project being described, these documents feel very familiar to an experienced bid manager. All the same elements are there: summary from the bid leader, vision and concept statements, features, benefits, differentiators, budgets, outline project plans, artists' impressions, flowcharts, structure charts...

You can see the work that went into constructing these books: one can only imagine the number of meetings that would have been needed to eventually determine the sheer level of detail covered on such a wide range of themes. In fact, Magliano concurs that the only way to manage the exchange of information between the team members was meeting after meeting. Concerns over the security of information meant that the team did not use storyboards or have a bid 'war room', so face-to-face briefings and updates were the way the team was kept up to date and on-message. To give an idea of the complexity of the technical bid, this phase took almost 18 months to complete.

Magliano acknowledges that, in any bid competition, the creation of the technical document, though necessary, will never win the competition for you (he does observe that a poor bid could create significant damage!). That said, the London 2012 bid was written to the highest possible standard and with the evaluators firmly in mind. He describes an effort to avoid a 'dry and dusty' written submission, but rather to write with 'clarity and simplicity', so that the evaluators wouldn't be frustrated by trying to find information. In addition, in recognition that some of the evaluators would not be reading the bid in their first language and that cultural differences existed across the panel, a certain style of international English would be required. In other words, the bid document was completely evaluator-focused, as all bid documents should be!

Listen and learn

The really critical phase was going to take place in the last six months of the bid, when the lobbying team and the marketing and communications team would go into overdrive to work on the stakeholders who would be involved either directly or indirectly in the voting that would take place on 6 July 2005.

In February 2005 a 13-strong delegation of IOC evaluators visited London for four days to see and hear for themselves exactly what London was offering. This visit had been planned and rehearsed over and over again and every eventuality had been considered and prepared for. In particular, the team knew that other candidate cities were pushing the concept that London's was a 'virtual bid', with the majority of the venues only at drawing board stage. Much was done to show real, on-the-ground work in progress, especially with regard to transport infrastructure – another known concern amongst the commissioners. This idea of addressing perceived weaknesses and showing them as actual strengths, was a very successful strategy. And the hosting, by the queen, of an evening dinner for the evaluation team at Buckingham Palace was a great way of promoting one of the bid's key strengths: the political backing of the bid by the head of state and her parliament – a very important consideration for the evaluating panel.

The public nature of the bid meant that every candidate city could access the feedback not only from their own evaluation visits but also from each of the others'. Despite very favourable reports from the commissioners, London was still perceived to be behind in the competition after the visits were complete.

Similarly, come May 2005, the evaluation of the technical bids was published – and each team could now see how it was placed in relation to the others. This kind of information is dynamite (imagine knowing before your final presentation how much ground you needed to make up!). London had acted on the feedback from the very first round of information submitted and evaluated back in 2004, and its technical bid received marks that moved them up the rankings. But, whilst the New York and Moscow bids were losing ground, Paris and Madrid had also strengthened their positions.

Armed with this new knowledge, and ready to use the information that had been quietly gathered on the preferences and opinions of the final decision makers, the 105 members of the IOC, Magliano and the rest of the team set to work on implementing their plans for the final month.

Influence and persuade

On the matter of influencing the final decision makers in the lead-up to the final presentation and voting, David Magliano is adamant about the need to get this phase right. When I somewhat clumsily suggested that the 'average' bid team would not have to worry about lobbying, he was quick to disagree. In every bid there will be influencers' doors to knock on, he (diplomatically) chided. I don't disagree; it's just that the doors aren't always clearly marked, and are often locked even if you can find them. In Olympic bidding, the ultimate decision makers are a visible (if not easily accessible) group, and engaging with them directly and indirectly can (and did in this case) make the difference between winning and losing.

One month before the presentations and voting session, the London team unleashed a very well-briefed, very powerful lobbying team that included, amongst others, Tony and Cherie Blair, the then Mayor of London Ken Livingstone, former Olympic and Paralympic champions, and David Beckham, at the time captain of the England football team. Led by Sebastian Coe, the Chairman of the London bid and himself a legendary Olympian, the lobbying was a scrupulously planned, tightly coordinated, highly targeted process, designed to cement the opinions of supporters and change the minds of 'floating' voters.

I have to say that it was this part of my discussion with David Magliano that affected me most of all. The power of London's strategy of understanding the ultimate audience, and of executing a precision campaign to persuade and influence them, is evident in the results of the final voting. The London team had done their homework and had not shied away from knocking on proverbial doors. I think this is a central learning point for any bid manager: keep influencing; don't hope that your technical document and final presentation will be enough. Keep doing things to ensure that your messages are being received loud and clear by your ultimate decision makers. Keep knocking on those doors.

The final presentation

And so to the final day of the bid – 6 July 2005, in Singapore. In a very familiar fashion, bidders were to have 45 minutes to make their final presentation to the panel. (This seems to be a fixed occurrence throughout the bid world: however large your bid, you'll always get 45 minutes to present it to the panel!)

It was the final chance to win over any voters who were still open to persuasion. The presentation needed to stand out from the others. It needed to home in on the one factor that would convince wavering members of the electorate that London was the right choice.

Before this could be done, David Magliano needed his team to recognize each of the core characters in the final act: the electorate, the London bid, and the four other candidate cities. Each 'character' had to be fully understood, plotted and accommodated into the script.

So, for the electorate, factors like geopolitical alliances, language expectations and cultural preferences had to be known and addressed. For competitors, their strengths and weaknesses thus far and the resulting likely bid themes and central messages had to be mapped out. Finally, London's own 'killer' premise was needed. David Magliano explains how he and his team finally arrived, after much debate and deliberation, at the central theme for the presentation.

They were looking for the point of overlap between the three needs of a winning presentation: to be compelling, authentic and different. This overlap would create what he refers to as 'the sweet spot' (Figure 15.1).

FIGURE 15.1   The presentation sweet spot

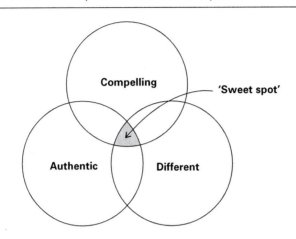

Magliano and his team would agonize long and hard to find their sweet spot. Eventually they agreed. London's would be this: their Games would inspire young people from around the world to participate in sports in the future as never before.

At this stage, Magliano admits that he was taking a risk. 'With this approach, we knew we'd either win or come last', he recalls. But, as London was the underdog in the competition, radical thinking was definitely required. Essentially, the way the presentation was to be developed would move the decision from the rational to the emotional. Recognizing that IOC members are custodians of the Olympic ideal, the presentation would focus on how the values and vision of the Olympic movement would be London's foremost consideration. History told Magliano that other bidding cities would treat the final presentation as a beauty parade, showing why they were the best city to act as hosts. Amazingly, this idea of the host city as a servant of the Olympic movement, rather than grateful beneficiary, had never been used as the central premise of a final presentation before.

With their sweet spot identified, the team began to work on how they would eventually present it, along with all the other core messages, in just 45 minutes in Singapore. What should be said, by whom, and how?

Magliano and his team eventually settled on a three-tier approach. The presentation would include:

1 *The technical:* an overview of the practical delivery of the London bid, but now focused on the 'why', not the 'how'. Magliano knew that this message needed to be seen, and that, although there were several extremely strong differentiators featured, they would not be enough to sway those who were still open to persuasion.

2 *The magic of London:* a showcase of the city. Magliano was confident that this would be the central theme chosen by the other bidders: that they would try to appeal to the electorate by demonstrating why and how their city was better than the other candidates. Again, he knew this message must be included – indeed it would be expected – and would provide reassurance that London was indeed a superb candidate city.

3 *Inspiration:* how London would take up the challenge to create a love of sport for young people all over the world. This message of inspiration was to be London's killer differentiator. In a highly charged and completely personal summation, Sebastian Coe would share how his own early inspiration led him to become an Olympic champion and, eventually, Chairman of the London bid. He would explain how the London Games would, through the similar inspiration of today's young people, safeguard the continual building of the Olympic ideal, and would ensure a lasting sporting legacy for future generations. Since many IOC members had themselves been Olympic competitors and could recall the source of their own inspiration, and since many now saw themselves as custodians of the Olympic cause, this approach was supremely unifying and very effective. It would encourage voters to rise above personal preferences and ensure that their decision would help to overcome one of the enduring challenges of the Olympic movement: the creation of a lasting legacy for young people.

As much as he needed the right messages, Magliano needed the right people to deliver them, and much was done to ensure that those selected to be part of the presentation would be able to get their point across effectively. What this actually meant was a punishing rehearsal schedule and the continual refining of the script to suit the presenters' individual styles.

Studying the final presentation in detail I am full of admiration for the way that the messages were scripted and delivered. I would encourage you to read the transcript, which can be found at **http://www.london2012.com/ documents/locog-publications/singapore-presentation-speeches.pdf**. This is what a world-class presentation looks like. For a really detailed look at the meaning behind the messages, and an insight into the logic and thinking behind each part of the script, I'd recommend that you read the final chapter of Jon Steel's *Perfect Pitch* (2007). If you'd like to watch it, for full impact, a film of the presentation can still be found on the *BBC News* website: look for the video clip entitled 'London's presentation' at **http://news.bbc.co.uk/ sport1/hi/other_sports/olympics_2012/4654821.stm**.

One last task remained, though. The presentation team would also have to face a Q&A session at the end of the presentation (again, a very familiar scenario to any bid manager). Any final stumbling blocks needed to be identified and prepared for in advance. No doubt could be introduced at this stage; no mistakes could be made. Again, Magliano's preparation was exemplary. His strategy here was to brief everyone on the questions they would answer, if asked. Every possible subject was prepared for. Sebastian Coe would acknowledge the question and hand it on to the predetermined subject-matter expert. No one would be allowed to 'chip in' and add to an answer, even if the expert was off-message. One question, one answer. In the event, the questions asked were easily handled, but Magliano's approach is one that we should all adopt forthwith.

After two years of shaping and refining the vision, it was finally complete. David Magliano's final day in the bid team (win or lose, his job was complete on 6 July 2005) was going to be one of the most important of his career, but all he could do was watch and wait. Such is the lot of the bid manager.

The decision

Nothing beats the feeling of winning a bid, and, despite Magliano's inevitable feelings of doubt in the hours between the presentation and the live televised announcement on 6 July 2005, he recalls the emotion the moment he realized that his strategy had worked. As Jacques Rogge, the President of the IOC, seemed to struggle with opening the envelope, and made the announcement 'The International Olympic Committee has the honour of announcing that the Games of the 30th Olympiad are awarded to the city of... London', Magliano and the rest of the team present in the Singapore Convention Centre on that evening could barely believe their ears. Going into the hall to hear the decision, Magliano felt pessimistic, ranking London's chances of winning at no better than 50:50.

Not even the media pack had expected London to win, and most had to sprint across the room from their position in front of the Paris team to capture the celebrations. 'It was such an intense feeling, and I cannot ever imagine experiencing such concentrated emotion ever again', Magliano explains.

Even now, watching footage of that moment and of the celebrations in Trafalgar Square makes you realize just how important the London 2012 bid team's efforts were. They had no guarantees, and had been standing in Paris's shadow, right from the start. But to me this is the finest and most inspiring lesson of all: underdogs can and do win. Prepare well and never give up. Then enjoy the rewards of your efforts.

Postscript

Of course, the jubilation felt by the bid team and people around the UK came to an abrupt end within 24 hours of the awarding of the Games to London. The 7/7 bombings shattered the mood and plunged the city into chaos for a while. Who could imagine whether the outcome would have been different if these tragic events had happened 48 hours earlier?

In my mind, the events of the day after are now inextricably entwined with the awarding of the Games to London. And it seems to me that the eventual mood that emerged, of resolve and renewed strength, only enhanced the vision of inspiration that the team worked so hard to create.

Now, after the Games, which were declared an overwhelming success around the world, we can perfectly see how the bid's central themes came to life and were delivered so superbly. How fantastic it must now be to know that you helped to imagine and to propose the model for this success in the first place.

Lessons every bid manager can learn from the London 2012 bid team

The story of the London bid, then, is an inspirational and memorable one, but does it truly offer opportunities for learning in bids operating on a much smaller scale and with far fewer resources? I absolutely believe it does. Below are the messages that came across loud and clear in my research into the London 2012 bid, in key areas.

On the decision to bid

Take time to make the right decision, considering the balance of risk in areas you can and can't control. Once you decide to participate, give it your all, and make sure there is a strong leader in place to deliver the bid and protect your investment in the process.

On preparing to bid

Make sure you give yourself time to prepare and plan before any real bidding work commences. The London team spent a huge proportion of their time on this stage.

Acknowledge that stakeholders will want to see early progress, but manage their expectations carefully.

Your competitors are in the same boat as you in terms of time. What other factors might improve your bid in relation to theirs? Skills training? Access to stakeholders? More resources? Get in shape.

On research

You cannot win a bid without research. Creating your own pitch without the knowledge of the rest of the marketplace is a very risky strategy. How can you identify differentiators if you don't know what others are offering? A good bid will take competitive pitches into consideration, and will flex accordingly, promoting benefits, addressing your own weaknesses, playing up others' weaknesses and identifying true differentiators.

You're unlikely ever to get the same kind of access to competitor information that the London bid team got, but over time you should be aiming to build as complete a picture as you can.

On creating your vision

Ideally, begin to develop a 'win theme' from the outset, and then ensure your technical team designs the solution with this in mind. If, as in the London bid, your technical solution emerges first, then make time as soon as possible to identify the benefits and possible differentiators that might be embedded within that solution. However you arrive at it, you must aim for the 'sweet spot' that David Magliano so skilfully deployed as the killer differentiator of the final presentation – every time.

On creating your technical bid

It's all right to fashion the elements of your operational solution into a customer-centred vision if that's how it emerges. The London team demonstrated that this can be an extremely effective model. But the relationship between your sales and operational teams is a vital one, and each must understand and be willing to cooperate with the other to bring together the winning proposal. Your internal teams need to be in constant communication to ensure that they are fully aware of the relationship between the technical elements and the messages that are being promoted.

Your written document is vital. It can't always win the competition for you; the final decision might be made on the power of your personal representation to the decision makers. But give it your all; give them no reason to raise a red flag against your operational proposal. And write it for your audience.

On listening, learning and lobbying

It's unlikely that you'll benefit from mid-process evaluations or feedback as the candidates in this process did, but there are ways of gauging the mood and determining whether you are largely on-track. Interact with your buying contact as much as possible. Participate fully in supplier briefing sessions and written question processes. Identify sympathetic 'coaches' within the buying organization and run things past them, if permitted. Undertake end-user research to test the reaction to your proposed solution.

The London team used all the historical information available to them as well as learning from the evaluation feedback given at key stages of the process. Using all this knowledge, they crafted their lobbying strategy, spending time on research and preparation well before unleashing their carefully chosen lobbying team. It was no accident that the right conversations took place between the right people at precisely the right moments.

In your own bids, the influencing of decision makers and other stakeholders must be managed carefully and in a compliant way – but use whatever means are available to inform, persuade and influence, either directly or indirectly.

And of course, at the end of any competition, ask for feedback, whether you win or you lose. You'll need this vital information for all of your future bids.

On preparing for the final presentation

David Magliano was clear from the start that the construction of the final presentation was perhaps the most important stage of the bid process. Take this view in your own bids. Everything you have done up until this point has been to secure your place on the final shortlist. You couldn't have won it before now, only lost it. You now have to convince your decision makers that you are the right choice. So:

- Prepare your messages.
- Select your presenters.
- Rehearse, refine, rehearse.

Prepare for the worst-case scenario in the Q&A – for all those questions you'd hate them to ask. Allocate subject-matter experts. One person answers each question – no chipping in allowed.

Oh, and did I mention rehearsing?

On winning

Enjoy it. Who knows what the next day will bring? Make sure you use your new experience, your new-found knowledge and your improved skills to make your next bid a winner as well.

The bad – techniques to avoid

In my conversations with other bid managers over the years, I've come across lots of examples of good practice. Everyone's happy to talk about the last brilliant bid they worked on, and where and how they've created success. But these discussions somehow never turn to the times when things haven't gone quite so well. Logic dictates that for every winner there is at least one loser in any competition – normally a lot more. I do accept that, just because your bid didn't win, it doesn't mean it was no good, but I was curious to try to find out what skeletons were lurking in those bid cupboards. I wanted to find out about the times when bids went wrong!

I've got some pretty horrible bid memories myself, of times when things have not gone to plan or have somehow come off the rails. What follows is a mixture of personal experience, stories that I have heard on the grapevine and anecdotes and tales that my fellow bid managers from around the world have shared with me. Many thanks to members from the APMP and from various bid-related discussion groups on LinkedIn. If I used your story, I've included your details in the Acknowledgements section at the beginning of this book.

The last-minute rewrite

There was the time that my boss, the sales lead, reviewed progress on a bid for a new piece of work with an existing client with 24 hours to go. He declared that the solution proposed was not what the client now wanted and that the bid did not address the client's vision and challenges. He promptly demanded a complete rewrite. The only thing that survived his red pen from my original 100-page draft was a single page of a case study. That was pretty demoralizing, I have to say. The rewrite was awful: a (new) solution that hadn't been worked through; insufficient detail in the response; inconsistent writing style; bad presentation; a commercial solution with glaring errors. A very ugly bid indeed.

Lesson? We should have made the decision not to bid after that bad review. (Actually, it should never have got to the stage where the bid lead felt that the solution was so far off track that it needed a rewrite.) Good leadership, planning and bid disciplines would have avoided the embarrassment of having to receive the client's feedback, and the demoralizing effect the whole process had on the team. From that day on, I never allowed anyone in a bid team to write anything until we were all clear on the win theme and had put a storyboard together.

The missed deadline

In the course of my research I came across many variations on this very familiar theme. Every single bid manager I know has their own set of stories about deadlines that they have actually or nearly missed. The universal truth about bidding is that there's never enough time and the deadline always comes around too fast.

Here are a few tales for you to learn from:

- One bid manager told me how a 200-page proposal that had taken several weeks to prepare was due at the client's offices in the week between Christmas and New Year. Finishing the document on Christmas Eve, the sales lead had left it in the post tray to go out via Royal Mail, thinking that there was plenty of time for it to arrive. However, because of bank holidays, the document arrived the day after the deadline and was duly returned unopened.

- In another case, a bid manager from the United States tells about the time his boss had chartered a light aircraft to fly a multi-volume bid from his company's offices to the customer's city location. Imagine his boss's distress when, on arriving at the airfield, he realized that the boxed-up and sealed packages containing the binders were too large for the small aircraft door! I gather it was a long drive throughout the night to get them there on time.

- Nearer to home and using a more familiar means of delivery, another bid team was working on a bid for HMP (Her Majesty's Prison) in Newport, South Wales. The courier picked up the document, which of course had been carefully prepared and all instructions followed. Checking with the courier the next day, the team was horrified to discover that the parcel had indeed been delivered on time – but to HMP at Newport, Isle of Wight.

I'm sure I don't need to point out the lesson here. Just don't leave anything to chance during your precious document's journey from your office to the client's.

The missed electronic deadline

Many a bid manager has fallen into the trap of thinking that an electronic bid submission via an e-procurement website will be much easier, without the hassle of the production and delivery of a hard-copy document. Not so!

I remember once working on a very large, very important bid that required all the documents to be uploaded via a procurement website. Knowing that sometimes these sites run very slowly as the clock ticks down the final hour (because suddenly all the bidders are trying to upload everything at the same time), I had everything loaded except one final document. But, try as I might, it just would not go on. At five minutes to go, a little crowd had gathered by my desk (everyone had some useful advice to offer) and the sales lead was on the phone to the client pleading our case. However, the client was adamant; all documents had to go via the website, which would be taken down at the precise moment the deadline passed. The document finally loaded with just 11 seconds to go. Fortunately we won that bid, but I have been left with a fear and distrust of procurement websites ever since!

In a similar vein, another bid manager recalls an instance where his team, having spent weeks putting a bid together, found that, after they had entered answers to all the questions online and hit 'Send', their submission failed. With minutes to go, the error message warned them that there were around 30 attachments missing. In this particular case, questions that seemed only to offer the option to attach a document actually required one to be present before it deemed the response complete. Frantically, the team, having provided a short response in the comments box for each of these questions, then attached blank letterheads to their answers just so that the submission could be pushed through the system.

The lessons here are clear. Make yourself familiar with the e-procurement system that the client is using. Attend the training seminar or take the online tutorial, even if you've used this particular application before. Test the process for uploading documents and read the instructions well before the final day. And most important of all – don't leave it until the last minute.

Inattention to detail

I've seen many a bid submitted with the name of another client included (the case against cut and paste) and other less calamitous 'typos' or mistakes that might just be overlooked, if you're lucky. But since a bid is supposed to represent your capability and credibility, don't expect a buyer to be too forgiving if you make the kinds of mistakes that have been confessed here.

The first involves a bid for a local authority that had two differing addresses within the ITT. One was a submission address and one was the address to which any questions or clarifications needed to be submitted. Unfortunately, the bid manager submitted the hard-copy bid to the 'questions' address. Not long afterwards, the bid reappeared on the sales director's desk with a note so say that it had been non-compliant and therefore disqualified. Cue a very difficult discussion between bid manager and boss!

During another public sector bid a different bid manager recalls that their package was entrusted to a professional courier company, which duly delivered the package on time and to the right destination. Unfortunately, as part of their standard practice for package processing, the courier had put a label on the box that included the name and address of the sender. The client rejected the bid because it breached the well-known public sector condition that tender packages must be unmarked and should not identify the bidding company in any way. In accordance with the rules, the package was sent back unopened.

I remember once hearing a story about a bid that went in without a final proofread, where under a section requesting historical performance management information a simple sentence had been inserted: 'Make something up to go in here!' I've heard many a variation on this particular theme, some much more cringe-worthy than this example, but the outcome will pretty much always be the same. The buyer won't be impressed and you will not win the bid.

In each of these cases, a little bit more time and attention to detail could have avoided an unhappy outcome. It's one thing for your competitors to put you out of the competition; it's another thing for you to do it to yourself!

The ugly – how not to do it

It's one thing to make a mistake inadvertently, and for your bid to go badly wrong despite your best efforts. But when you make a judgement call about how to play a bid and your thinking is flawed, well, things can just turn out plain old ugly.

The buyer is wrong

Time without number, I've come across sales people who read through a tender document and then declare: 'Well, that buyer's just not asking the right question!' They then plough on with writing a solution that is based on the answering of the 'right question', certain that the buyer will see the error of his or her ways after reading the submission. Guess what? Buyers have the ability to say no to proposals that don't meet their requirements. In every case like this that I've ever worked on, they have.

Alternatively, a sales lead might try to argue with the buyer that the evaluation criteria are wrong: too heavily weighted towards price, for instance, with insufficient weight given to quality. A sales lead once admitted to me that he had on one occasion got into an argument with a buyer about how a particular bid should be evaluated. Not surprisingly, his bid didn't win.

Lesson? Play it the buyer's way. Submit a variant bid by all means (answering what you believe to be the 'right' question or promoting the business case of your alternative solution), but first follow the buyer's original instructions and submit a compliant bid too. Otherwise I can guarantee that you'll find yourself out of the running.

Presentation team politics

A business development manager told me the tale of an 'ugly' presentation that he participated in many years ago. Within the presentation team were two somewhat opinionated individuals, a situation that often led to tension in their interactions. During the presentation one of the individuals answered a question, making some big promises concerning service delivery and communication. Unfortunately, the body language of the other individual made clear her disagreement to every promise he made. Needless to say the result was not a win and in the debrief the client cited politics and conflicts within the team as one of the main reasons for their decision.

It's so important to get the team right and to brief them on their exact role within the presentation. Leave nothing to chance, and rehearse until no doubts remain.

Presentation team gimmicks

One great anecdote I received is the classic illustration of how pride comes before a fall (quite literally). A few years ago, a property company pitched to developers to be office agents on a prestigious new London high-rise office building that would appear to be built entirely of glass. The company produced a scale-model ice sculpture of the building, proudly giving it centre stage in the meeting room during the final presentation. All was going well – so well in fact that the two-hour meeting drifted into a four-hour session. You can guess the rest. Down it came: melt-water all over the table, papers ruined, suits soaked. End of discussions!

You might be tempted to go for some kind of gimmick, either in the way you produce your bid submission or in the final presentation. But, before acting, think carefully, and put yourself in the buying team's shoes. How's this really going to look? Does it advance your cause or enhance your reputation? Play devil's advocate before making the final decision to proceed. If you want to be bold, be bold. Just don't be brash.

So there we have it: equal doses of the inspired and the imperfect, the brilliant and the botched. Most mistakes made on bids aren't as noteworthy as these. They normally involve misinterpreting a customer's requirements, or running out of steam, or making compromises to get the job done on time. Of course, you'll always make your own mistakes, but hopefully the lessons recorded in this chapter will remain with you as your bid experience builds.

SUMMARY

Think positively! Underdogs can (and do) win – but you need to be prepared for a tough and well-prepared fight if you're going to beat the odds.

Undertake as much research as you can. Don't be afraid to use a significant portion of the time available on research and in the planning of your bid strategy.

Ensure that you have a great internal dialogue going between your sales team and your operational team. Get them to work together towards a clearly identified vision.

The influencing of decision makers needs to be a key part of your strategy. Work out how you are going to get your messages through to them: within the rules, of course.

Get organized! Everyone makes mistakes, but try to do everything possible to eliminate those that are avoidable. Well before the pressure of the final day, hours and minutes of submitting your written bid and then making your final presentation, concentrate on all the little details that might otherwise undo all your efforts.

REFERENCES, FURTHER READING AND RESOURCES

Books

Lee, Mike (2006) *The Race For the 2012 Olympics*, Virgin Books, London
Newman, Larry (2006) *Proposal Guide for Business and Technical Professionals*, 3rd edn, Shipley Associates, Farmington, UT
Steel, Jon (2007) *Perfect Pitch*, Adweek Books, Hoboken, NJ

Government publications

Gershon, P (2004) *Releasing Resources to the Frontline: Independent review of public sector efficiency* (Gershon Review), July, HM Treasury, HMSO, Norwich
Glover, A (2008) *Accelerating the SME Economic Engine: Through transparent, simple and strategic procurement* (Glover Report), November, HM Treasury, London

Electronic sources

Electronic sources are given within the relevant chapters. Further sources include the following:

EC procurement thresholds as of 1 January 2012: http://www.ojec.com/threshholds.aspx

European Union common procurement vocabulary codes: see http://simap.europa.eu/codes-and-nomenclatures/codes-cpv/codes-cpv_en.htm

Freedom of Information Act: http://www.legislation.gov.uk/ukpga/2000/36/contents; http://www.direct.gov.uk/en/

Governmentcitizensandrights/Yourrightsandresponsibilities/
DG_4003239; http://www.whatdotheyknow.com; and
http://www.freedomofinformation.co.uk/

PAS91 information: http://shop.bsigroup.com/en/Navigate-by/PAS/
PAS-912010/

Procurement notices relating to UK government:
http://www.cabinetoffice.gov.uk/search/apachesolr_search/
procurement?filters=tid%3A1384

Remedies Directive: http://www.ojec.com/directives.aspx

Standard PQQ core questions: https://update.cabinetoffice.gov.uk/sites/
default/files/resources/Annex-A-Core-PQQ-questions.pdf

The Public Contracts (Amendment) Regulations 2009: see
http://www.opsi.gov.uk/si/si2009/uksi_20092992_en_1

The Public Contracts Regulations 2006: see
http://www.opsi.gov.uk/si/si2006/20060005.htm#23

UK government mystery shopper programme:
http://www.cabinetoffice.gov.uk/resource-library/
mystery-shopper-scope-and-remit

Other resources

There's a wealth of information out there if you'd like to further explore bidding best practice and keep improving your knowledge and skills.

APMP

If you're really serious about progressing as a bid management professional, then I heartily recommend that you consider joining the Association of Proposal Management Professionals. The APMP is 'the worldwide authority for professionals dedicated to the process of winning business through proposals, bids, tenders, and presentations'. It exists to promote 'the professional growth of its members by advancing the arts, sciences, and technologies of winning business'.

I've been a member since 2006 and can honestly say that it transformed my approach to my role, inspiring me to keep learning about global best practice and to apply this learning in every bid.

The APMP runs a three-level accreditation programme that assesses your skills, knowledge and experience and allows you to demonstrate the level of competency to which you are operating. I proudly hold second-stage accreditation (Practitioner level). The first level is Foundation; the third is Professional. I'm just trying to find time to get to that stage!

The APMP is based in the United States, but has a thriving UK chapter. There are loads of opportunities to get involved, to meet other bid managers outside of live competitions (which means that you can actually talk to each other!) and to learn about the tools and techniques that are in use elsewhere in the bidding community.

For further information, see:

www.apmp.org
www.ukapmp.co.uk

LinkedIn

LinkedIn is a valuable resource for bid managers, whose roles can leave them a little isolated from others in the same position. It's difficult to meet others engaged in bids face to face, so this virtual approach can be a good solution.

If you're not sure that you want to go as far as full APMP membership, you might want to get a taster of the type and quality of knowledge to which you'd have access by joining the lively bid and proposal management community on LinkedIn.

APMP and UKAPMP both have their own groups, but there are lots of others that you can join. If you look through the discussions, you'll see just how much information and debate is exchanged through this forum. I find it really useful, and try to contribute whenever I can.

For insight into procurement thinking and advancements, I'm also a member of a number of groups aimed at buyers, and would recommend that you observe what they're discussing too!

INDEX

NB: page numbers in *italic* indicate figures or tables

CPSIA information can be obtained at www.ICGtesting.com
Printed in the USA
BVOW010857060513

319982BV00002B/2/P